Stop Dreaming and Start Renovating for Profit

Stop Dreaming and Start Renovating for Profit

A Guide to Building Wealth
through Property Renovations

Rebeka Morgan

WILEY

First published 2025 by John Wiley & Sons Australia, Ltd

© John Wiley & Sons Australia, Ltd 2025

The right of Rebeka Morgan to be identified as the author of *Stop Dreaming and Start Renovating for Profit* has been asserted in accordance with law.

ISBN: 978-1-394-27129-0

A catalogue record for this book is available from the National Library of Australia

Registered Office
John Wiley & Sons Australia, Ltd. Level 4, 600 Bourke Street, Melbourne, VIC 3000, Australia

For details of our global editorial offices, customer services, and more information about Wiley products visit us at www.wiley.com.

Wiley also publishes its books in a variety of electronic formats and by print-on-demand. Some content that appears in standard print versions of this book may not be available in other formats.

Cover design by Wiley
Cover and page images: © Jane Kelly/Adobe Stock

Figure 2.8/2.9 material photos: (c) jokerpro/Adobe Stock; Africa Studio/Adobe Stock; aopsan/Adobe Stock; Ahmad TB/Adobe Stock; Shawn Hempel/Adobe Stock

Set in Neulis Sans 10pt/13pt by Straive, Chennai, India.
Printed and bound by CPI Group (UK) Ltd, Croydon, CR0 4YY

C9781394271290_150325

Contents

About the author

Rebeka Morgan is a dedicated mother, experienced renovator, registered builder and seasoned property developer. She is the founder of BuildHer Collective, a business designed to empower and support women in the building industry — whether they are constructing their own homes or developing for profit.

With a background in quantity surveying (specialising in cost management), project management and commercial construction, Rebeka brings a wealth of expertise to the residential property development space. She made the decision to leave her role as general manager of a commercial building company to spend more time with her family and create her own path in residential development.

For over a decade, renovating for profit and managing projects has been central to Rebeka's career. She has successfully completed a diverse range of projects, including new builds, renovations, subdivisions, vineyard refurbishments and joint ventures. Her extensive experience spans various property styles and project types, demonstrating her adaptability and expertise in transforming spaces for both residential and investment purposes.

Introduction

Renovating houses, buying and selling has been an amazing gift for me and my family. We, our family, have had immense benefits from playing and operating in this space. With seven children, we have been able to navigate the many changes of life and time constraints, and have had the gift of flexibility in playing in a non-traditional space. While my first renovations were completed when I was working fulltime, since then we have been able to focus on building a business alongside building houses, first working for people and then moving to doing our own projects.

I work alongside my wonderful, generous and handsome partner John, whom I met on one of my first renovations, when I hired him to do some work for me. Now we both work on projects together and separately. He is my rock and safe place — he is generally the voice of reason when I have another crazy idea or want to take on another project that we don't have time for. We have found our rhythm together over the years, built trust and an ease about the work we do. We still have moments for sure (every project has a nib wall we don't agree on) but as a whole we challenge each other, making the process less lonely and way more fun.

I do not have a get-rich-quick program for you — a pathway to making money without effort — but throughout this book you will find the systems, processes and theory that I have been honing while building and renovating. I have helped countless people renovate and build personally and through my BuildHer Collective community and I want you to keep in mind that this will be a journey, both physically and emotionally. Rarely will people buy, renovate and sell without having to overcome challenges, without having moments of doubt, without occasionally getting overwhelmed. If it were easy and straightforward you wouldn't need a book and everyone would be doing it, but then there probably wouldn't be any profit in it either.

BuildHer Collective is a business I created to help women renovate their own homes. At the time I was building houses with my partner John and we were being contacted by many friends and friends of friends who had issues in their build. Many times (most times) the problems that were causing so much grief and angst were avoidable. There were simple steps that could have led to a much better outcome, and the problem wasn't always with the builder, but there was always an element of miscommunication involved. With the right training or help in the beginning these were avoidable. The other thing that kept coming up was that people didn't know what they didn't know, so they were making decisions without a complete understanding of the process or what impact the decisions were making further down the track. However, it was no one person's job to help someone, there were no rules or independent places you could go to get advice or learn how to manage the process properly. And when you are spending hundreds of thousands of dollars, and your life savings, this is craziness. This prompted the idea of BuildHer Collective, which helps women build.

The second thing that BuildHer is now known for, again, stemmed from people asking for help. As John and I were renovating for profit and had tested a number of ways to do this, we were getting questions and asks about how other people could renovate and sell for a profit too. Now, I never wanted to have a business or any relationship with 'flipping houses' or 'developing' as they always felt cheap — it felt somehow dirty and like it wasn't ethical. But I began to realise that the 'want' to renovate for profit or flip houses is not actually about this. It is about creating something that someone else will live in, it's about creating an income that is physical and tangible in a world where it can feel like we are just pushing about paper and emails, and it is about creating a life and lifestyle that fits in with your values. This I could get behind. This did not feel slimy or sleazy or like we were making money at the expense of the purchaser. This was the beginning of the DevelopHer Masterclass.

Throughout this book my focus will be to develop your skills in all areas of the build — there are many — and to support your forecasted profitable feasibility, turning it into realised profit. Building is really fun. Being creative and making a profit on your projects is really fun (way more fun than taking a loss!), but it requires skills and nuance.

Rising markets have given many renovators a false sense of security. They may have completed a renovation and increased the value of their property, but if land value rose by that same amount then they could have also done nothing and made the same return — which would have taken way less effort! We have all heard of someone that brought for x and sold for $1m more and the assumption was they made a million dollars. We are here to teach you that this is not the case. But if you do your numbers correctly and follow the guides, by the end of this book you will have a better understanding of capital improvement vs home improvement vs actual bankable profit.

I will teach you in this book how to look for areas where you can manufacture profit, how to put together a feasibility before you purchase — this will be your blueprint to making money — and how to then realise your profits by taking up the little 1 per cent gains that can add up to tens of thousands — if not hundreds of thousands — of dollars along the way!

I want you to know that while each project has its challenges, rarely do people get to the end without having fun, without a massive sense of accomplishment and without learning a lot about themselves and the process. This is a game where you will always be learning. In the start you might be learning the process, but then it will be the nuance, the systems and the structures that make this game so fun. I love the creativity of the process, from finding a new project, to exploring and designing a new home with different finishes, ideas and designs. What a gift to be able to create a home that someone will get to live in and share with their family and friends.

When you master the art of renovating for profit you will be able to adjust the types of projects you do around your life and lifestyle, depending on what this season brings you: a quick internal renovation one year and a larger dual occupancy the rest. I have liked to run a number of projects at one time and then take a break. We have had six-month breaks between projects where, as a family, we have been able to travel and live in our own little bubble. We are always learning and adjusting what serves to do and what suits us at the time. Our family changes and has different needs as they grow which can be factored into our lifestyle and, as we build we learn and adapt along the way.

In the past few years, we have had so many successful stories from our BuildHer Collective students — too many to mention — but here are just a few that come to mind as I write this:

- Taeler made $230000 on her first renovation in 10 months while on maternity leave and has not had to return to work as she is moving from project to project.
- Joni made a healthy amount selling her single-fronted Victorian house in Brunswick and went all in on the next house, making $2 million from this one project.
- Anna made $500000 on a knock-down rebuild while having babies.
- Mel made $57000 on an apartment renovation that took just 6 weeks.
- Elise made $880000 on a home that she renovated in stages while working fulltime.
- Hannah sold her attached home for a whopping profit, moving into the dream mid-century home that would never have been on the horizon for her, sparking a change of career.
- Tyler was able to quit her job and start her own business from the sale of her renovated passive house property, moving into a gorgeous 1950s heritage home.
- Rachel renovated and sold homes quickly using a seller joint-venture model, one of which took $50000 of work to create $450000 of profits and is on her 4th project now.

Everyone's story is unique to them in the way they use their projects to align with their life goals, values and interests. I am so excited and privileged to be working with so many incredible women and hope I get to share in some of your adventures and wins too. Our whole team would love to hear about your wins if you email us at info@buildhercollective.com.au.

I always loved property, but never thought I would be able to make a living this way. I am still surprised and grateful that we took the plunge and made the decision to give it a go. Those turning-point moments — the sliding doors moments — are still so clear in my mind. We have had a huge amount of freedom afforded to us, along with a complete adventure through embarking on this journey. I don't know what your journey will hold for you, but I hope it will be as amazing and as fun as ours has been.

1

Building courage: it's all about mindset

Renovating, building and developing for profit is actually more a mindset game than anything else. Most of us understand the concepts of housing and improving value and while we might not know all of the ins and outs we do understand that:

— everyone needs somewhere to live

— over time property will increase in value.

In Australia, our home is our haven, our safety net, and many of us have been brought up with the great Australian dream of owning property — specifically, owning property that offers a passive rental income as well as capital growth.

We know we need to build wealth and that the way to do this is to invest (more to come on this topic). However, 2024 data from Michael Yardney's website *propertyupdate.com.au* reveals that only 20 per cent of Australians own an investment property. Within that 20 per cent the split looks like this:

— 71.5 per cent of investors hold one investment property

— 18 per cent of investors hold two investment properties

— 9.7 per cent of investors hold three, four or five investment properties

— 0.8 per cent (or 19 895) investors hold six or more investment properties.

To compound this issue, women are behind in the property ownership stakes.

So, if we understand the concept of investing and wealth creation, why are more of us not acting? The primary constraints that people tell us about at BuildHer Collective are:

— *time to work on a project* — we are all so busy

— *money* — capital to invest

— *knowledge* — knowing what to do!

Now, when you look at the investment percentages quoted above take into account renovations and developments for short-term profit; however, most of them will be long-term holding properties.

Long-term investing is the topic for another book. Our focus here will be to look at strategies to effectively manufacture growth and wealth through property development and renovation to increase the value of your property in order to build your wealth and capital quickly. Or relatively quickly, I should say, as I don't teach or preach quick, low-return flips, which are both exhausting, and risky when you have an educated buyer pool. We will introduce you to the skills that you need to develop properties, but this is only a snapshot of each area you will need to be knowledgeable in. Each project you complete has a range of scenarios and problems to solve, there is no one size fits all. What we teach is how to ask the right questions and to have a base level understanding which enables you to seek answers.

I will be looking at ways you can renovate for profit — that is, increase the sale price of a property by adding real value, strategically. There are many ways you can do this, including:

— cosmetic renovations

— structural renovations and extensions

— changing the use of a property

— subdivision

— plans and permits.

But before I begin with the detail, I need to start with the big picture. Why are you here and what are you looking to gain during this process?

Goals and financial planning

In this game, it's the destination that so many people lack a vision for.

What is the destination for you? I know we all often talk about what our goals are for the next year or 5 years, but what is the end game here if we start earlier? Is this only something that becomes important enough to think about when you have just 5 or 10 years up your sleeve before you retire? Or perhaps you might want to start the game early, when you have time to action it.

One of my favourite games is to imagine and plan what will be 'enough'. And yes, this is different for everyone. And no, I don't care if you are greedy here and you let your mind wander ... what I do care about is the 'why' and the action plan.

But what is all this effort and planning ahead for?

For me and my family this is about knowing that we will be protected and have enough money to enjoy our future. To be able to look after not just ourselves but our children too. To know that we can age without the stress of money, and have the freedom of time. I love showing other people (especially women) that some of these concepts are not difficult, that a little effort will give a big reward. I also think there is so much competing noise that it can be hard to plan for the future when current lifestyle pressures are already a lot. We like to challenge the accepted norms that somehow we buy into without realising that we are doing so.

Are you going to spend your life working to pay off your home and then live off your super, which is controlled by the government? Are you planning to live off the age pension?

Here is the game: the 'What do I want and what do I need?' game. And there is a genuinely logical way to play it. Get ready to make your financial plan, my friends.

This financial plan is a simple one that doesn't factor in everything. It is not a replacement for a financial planner, nor is it a comprehensive plan; however, it will be a plan to get you started and to get you thinking!

Why do I love this? Because it is a base — something to build on — and it is so much better than the lack of a plan that most people have.

Your planning begins with a couple of questions. I'd like you to answer them quickly and without overthinking — you can always come back to them later if you want to revise and rethink your answers.

Answer these questions to work out a simple calculation:

— What is the value of the home I imagine living in (X)?

— What is the passive income I want to earn per year (Y)?

Now, divide the income (Y) by 5 per cent, and add the value of your home (X):

Y / 5 per cent + X = the total assets you will need.

Let's work it out

— The value of the home I want to live in is $1.5 million.

— The passive income I want to earn, as a family, is $200 000 per year.

Here is the calculation (the result of this calculation is called the 'total asset base'):

Income	$200 000 / 5%	$4 000 000
Value of home		$1 500 000
Total asset base to reach financial freedom		$5 500 000

Now, do we know that we will get a 5 per cent return on my investments? No. It will depend on how you invest your money — that is, the outgoings and incomings. Your investments could be, and probably should be, a mix of shares and property. You will also want to deduct inflation from this stat, and, of course, the growth in the asset price would not be realised unless or until you sell the property. There are many factors — which you will need to work through when you are in wealth preservation mode — but for now let's just keep things basic to give ourselves a goal.

While we're talking about shares and property, here are some stats for you to ponder. The *savings* website reported that over the 20 years to December 2017, Australian shares averaged returns of 8.8 per cent per year, while returns on Australian residential property averaged 10.2 per cent per year. The annual inflation rate over that period of time averaged 2.47 per cent. So once you have earned the money, you can create a plan to passively grow it — and both shares and property seem good options based on those numbers.

Now that you have calculated your total asset base, let's change things up a bit.

Dare to dream of how it might be!

Let's say the value of the home you live in is $3 000 000 and the value of your non-income-producing holiday house is $2 000 000.

Let's assume you'd like an income that will allow you to have freedom, not think about money and travel the world — say $500 000 per year.

If we work through the above calculation, we end up with:

Income	$500 000 / 5%	$10 000 000
Non-income producing assets		$5 000 000
Total asset base to reach financial freedom		$15 000 000

Add the two amounts together to get $15 000 000 worth of assets, mortgage free. (Remember, you need to be mortgage free on your home so that it is not adding to your repayment load and allows for all of your income to be channelled into fun.)

Yes, friends, this is simplistic, but without having a crystal ball we need to plan where we are heading and what we want to achieve without getting stuck into the minutia. Along the way, we will adjust the figures as we close in on our goals to reflect the reality of your situation.

I'd now like you to ponder these questions:

— *How does this make you feel?* Is it overwhelming and hard to imagine? Is it calming to have a goal and something on the horizon that you can plan towards? Is it motivating to get stuck in right now and start playing the game, knowing that every time you start out you need to learn a skill that you can then leverage to get ahead?

— *What are you going to do about this?* One of the best ways I know of to increase an asset base significantly is to renovate for profit. Now, you don't need to necessarily sell the asset at the end of the renovation to realise the profit, but it is a way to add big chunks of capital and to start to close the gap between where you are now and your end game!

Pro tip

Have a family meeting and work through this exercise with your significant other. If there is no 'other', work through it with a friend and think about how you can get to your end result. Scott Pape, the Barefoot Investor, recommends some version of a financial date night each month with your significant other. This is a great way to start planning, align your goals and make finances a fun game that you can work through together.

Being a Master BuildHer or DevelopHer

What does 'renovating for profit' or being a DevelopHer mean to you?

When you hear the term 'property developer', what mental image does it conjure up for you?

— Is it someone who builds large, multi-residential buildings?

— Do they take care or cut corners?

— Are you picturing a male or a female?

— Are they cutthroat, ruthless and shrewd? Do they have a lot of money?

— Are they the type of person you imagine yourself being? Someone you would aspire to be?

The *Cambridge Dictionary*'s definition of property developing is 'the process of buying, improving, and selling buildings and land, and arranging for new buildings to be built'.

With this in mind, I want you to think again about what it would mean to be a property developer: to renovate for profit; to improve buildings for others to use; to buy and sell property; to organise, design and plan for new buildings to be built.

At BuildHer Collective we have coined the person you just created a 'DevelopHer': a woman who renovates, improves and develops property. Someone who considers the best use and outcome of a space and building and who plans to improve it functionally and aesthetically as well as financially.

Our natural bias, labels and associations, and the way we imagine the world in terms of stereotypes, can stop us from wanting to succeed. They can limit our thinking and ideas of success and minimise the amazing wins we might have along the way.

If your picture of someone who is 'wealthy' — of someone who is a 'successful property developer' — has a negative bias, then your desire to follow this path might be wavering. Your negative bias might prevent you from wanting to succeed, tackle a project or be financially successful — because surely that would mean you were cutting corners and profiteering, right? Or perhaps it's that you have had success but you don't count these projects as successes, citing luck as the reason you've been successful, thereby minimising your skills, effort and thoughtfulness in this area. If that's you, you need to shift your mindset right now.

In this book what I am really looking to do is show you why renovating for profit, or developing, is a great way to build wealth fast and how you too can build your wealth by building or renovating and adding value using property.

Where to start

The fundamentals I will be covering are really important. There's no point jumping into tips and tricks and quick wins if you don't understand the basics.

Essentially, the formula is to buy a property, renovate it, then sell said property for more than the purchase price and costs.

The premise you need to understand to do this is:

— know what to buy and why (This is all about understanding feasibilities)

— do the work and build wealth by adding value

— sell for a profit — then rinse and repeat.

The truth is, I can make it as simple as possible for you, but there will be nuances. You will need to use your judgement and your powers of deduction when carrying out a renovation.

For starters, you will need to know:

— how much it will cost to buy the property you want to renovate

— the scope of works needed to add value on a budget

— how much the scope of works will cost and what the return on investment will be

— how to finance the build efficiently

— for how much, and how, you will sell the property.

As I unpack each of the above steps, you will realise that there are many different ways to work out and complete each one. But, instead of finding this daunting, I would encourage you to see it as exciting. A hobby, a skill, but most importantly FUN!

This is why we're here! This is why you are reading this book: so you have the smarts to make decisions on the process and put into practice all of your learnings, based not just on gut feel but on market research and budgets that will let you know before you begin that the project is worth spending your time and money on.

Big picture to project planning

To work out what projects you want to complete, you will need to look at the big picture, this helps you to really focus on where you need to be headed. One part of the big picture is capturing a snapshot of your life and how much you can realistically take on.

I will look at other big-picture aspects such as market forces later in the book.

But initially, if you are going to win at this game, you need to have a good look at your capacity, risk appetite, assets and values before you begin. Consider:

— How important is it for you to get started?

— What is your capacity to juggle another project on top of your existing work–life load?

— What does this mean about the type of project you can take on?

— How well do you handle unknowns — that is, what is your risk appetite?

— What assets and resources do you have access to? (cash/time/skills)

— What types of projects interest you?

Your driving force is a huge factor in whether or not you will make your dream a reality.

Here's a somewhat unfortunate reality: most people who buy this book will do nothing. A fair number of them will never reach this page. So, well done for making it this far!

So, how important is it to you to take action? What will change in your life if you start to renovate for profit and build your coffers for later in life?

Let me share with you some fun facts that might scare you into action:

— The Australian Government's Treasury office found that, in 2020, 70 per cent of women retiring did so with $250 000 in their super funds. Now, if you had to live off this alone and you had a consistent annual rate of 5 per cent return, that would give you $12 500 of income per year.

— The Australian Government's Treasury office also identified that, on average, women retire with only 70 per cent of the superannuation that men do. This is partially, but not wholly, due to women having children (though, frankly, I loved taking time off to have babies and wouldn't trade that for all the money in the world).

Now, if I flip this rhetoric and ask the question another way…
'How much do you want or need to live on per year when you
retire?'…this becomes a very interesting game — and the results
might surprise you.

To answer this, we'll assume, for simplicity, that you will receive a
5 per cent return (above inflation) on your investments and that you
own your own home.

Here's how to work it out

**[Amount I want to live on] / 5 per cent + value of my house =
amount I need in property and/or investments**

In other words, if you want $150 000 per year to live on
and the value of your house is $1.75 million, then the
calculation will be:

Amount I want to live on	$150 000
Amount I want to live on / 5 per cent	$3 000 000
Value of house/assets	+ $1 750 000
Amount needed in property/investments	$4 750 000

Or, if you want $50 000 per year to live on and your house is
worth $500 000, it would be:

Amount I want to live on	$50 000
Amount I want to live on / 5 per cent	$1 000 000
Value of house/assets	+ $500 000
Amount needed in property/investments	$1 500 000

Now let's say you and your family need $200 000 per year to
live on, and you own a home worth $2.5 million and a holiday
house worth $1.5 million:

Amount I want to live on	$200 000
Amount I want to live on / 5 per cent	$4 000 000
Value of house	+ $2 500 000
Value of holiday house	+ $1 500 000
Amount needed in property/investments	$8 000 000

The amount of equity you have in all your asset classes, including property, when you reach the end of your working career will determine the lifestyle you will be able to afford from this point forward. That total equity value can and should include things like shares, super, property and any other investments that can generate a passive income. You also need to allow for non-income-producing assets such as the home you live in, cars, cash at the bank, a holiday home, and so on. My partner and I calculate our requirements like this as most people we know like to own the property they live in, and we want to make sure we add this amount to the income-producing assets.

'Why do you focus on property?' you ask.

Simply because I know property. I don't know shares, so I can't teach you about them, but diversifying your assets is a good thing that someone more qualified than I am can demonstrate.

The other reason I have focused, and am focusing, on renovating for profit is because it's a way of adding bulk amounts of cash to your bottom line quickly. That way you make big jumps along your path to freedom. It's much harder to save your way to financial freedom.

Take for example, *finder*'s statistics, which reveal that the average Australian has only $37 975 in savings. Realistically, based on this, it's unlikely we will be saving our way to retirement. And with the ABS declaring in 2023 that an Australian woman's average annual wage is $87 714, it would take 75 years of saving $20 000 per year from this wage and adding it to your retirement fund to reach $1 500 000.

If you could do 10 renovations/extensions/developments, each totalling $150 000 profit after tax and each one taking 2 years, then over 20 years you would be adding $1 500 000 to your bottom line — and most people will do this on top of their regular income.

Sure, the reality is that no-one has a super smooth and easy journey. I have had projects that made $800 000 in profit in 18 months and we've also had joint-venture-style projects where investors contributed $200 000 and received a profit of $63 000 in 18 months.

The aim is to continually learn and grow. Not all projects will knock it out of the park with a home run, but if you do your numbers right, and understand feasibility and value propositions, you can make great returns and increase your family's wealth considerably.

As always, though, this is a game of time: time involved in the process, time to learn and time and effort spent 'doing'. I often ask the question, 'Where would you be now if you'd started 5 years ago?' The reality is, the first project or two can be a stretch. But as time goes on the compound effect makes it easier to play the game.

So, if you take one thing from this book, it would be to please get started. Start your journey of wealth creation and future financial security. You will be so much better off for it.

Juggling projects with your existing work–life load

It can be difficult to find time to focus on the big picture during our busy lives. Each project takes a different level of time investment. For joint ventures, you might invest money and then sit back and wait until your return materialises. Other projects might entail turning up 30 hours a week and getting physically involved with the renovations.

There are no rights or wrongs here in terms of the types of projects and what each produces, but there may be a wrong for you and your family if a project puts you under a time pressure that you deem isn't worth the sacrifice.

We, as a family, have undertaken many different types of projects. Some have been really hard to juggle; some have been great family projects where we have all become involved; and some have involved a couple of meetings, several emails — and ta-da! The deal's done.

While I was busy in the having babies stage of our life, our family had a 5-minute rule. That is, we wouldn't take on any project that was more than 5 minutes away from home. It was too far given the level of orchestrated chaos that was ensuing on a daily basis with six kids and two working parents (albeit both with very flexible, choose-you-own-adventure jobs).

Now that the kids are older, our framework has changed, but our holistic family values are still considered when we look at taking on a project. We don't tend to work weekends on projects where we are physically on-site building so we only build during the week, or we might hire a builder (yes, we are builders, but sometimes it's better to hire a builder to complete the work than overcommit our time)?

 ## Pro tip

Think about the type of project you're interested in taking on and anticipate your time requirements. Work out how you can fit it in and what peripheral or external resources (such as extended family help or childcare) you might need.

Here is a guestimate of the hours you'll need to put in:

— *Owner-building*: 30+ hours per week

— *Blended BuildHer*: approximately 20 hours per week. This is where you are working alongside a registered builder but still getting involved onsite and with ordering (more about this in chapter 6)

— *Managing a builder*: 2 to 10 hours per week, depending on your builder.

Other projects will be project dependent.

Let's take a look at what you'll need to consider if you're juggling work and family.

What does this mean about the type of project I can take on?

Be realistic about the type of project you can manage at the moment. Is this going to be one where you are onsite hiring trades, or one where you are best positioned to manage a builder?

What supports do you have available to help you manage the increased workload? Do you have family and/or friends you can call on? Do you have children who might need to be in care a few extra days a week, or could they stay overnight at Grandma and Grandpa's house when you need to make the final push?

Do you feel like you may be better off doing a project with someone more experienced for your first project? Or perhaps you might want to stagger the workload and start building your onsite team early?

How well do you handle unknowns?

Ahhh, we really do like a bit of a critical assessment of our capacity to handle problems and workshop them or to 'Chicken Little' where setbacks feel like the sky is falling down. Self-reflection is an amazing asset and it's worth taking a few moments to really think about your reactions and how you can put in place structures to help you handle these unknowns. Thinking about the worst-case scenario and how you might handle it will be a great help here!

What assets and resources (cash/time/skills) do you have access to?

I have found it helpful to write a list of all my back-up plans and the resources I have available to me should I need them. Resources can be in the form of many things, but money, time and skills are the biggest ones.

As far as money goes, ask yourself, 'What cash do I have available? What could I access if I had an issue? (Could I sell shares, access other money, borrow from family, leverage off a different asset in the short term, sell an asset like a car and get another lease? Pay for some things on the credit card? Transfer flybuys into cash rewards?' These are not the plan, but I like to understand my back-up plans — we all need a contingency plan.) I know of many situations where people have banded together to lend money or time temporarily. Most people are too proud to ask for or admit it, but we have all had help. Not many people are truly self-made.

In terms of time, how much time do I have to put into a project and what could I do if I needed more time? What could I stop doing for a few months? What help could I get to leverage my time if I needed to? Who might be able to help me?

I acknowledge that this is a privileged position, but I know that my amazing family would jump into action (and they have many times on previous projects). We are a family that would give the shirt off our back to each other. My mum has helped me run around looking at couches to style houses, cleaned, looked after kids, moved furniture and so much more. My dad has talked with me about potential projects — about things he has liked and not liked — talked through issues, provided guidance and a listening ear, loaned us money when I havon't budgeted properly, been there during our projects — and so much more. For our early projects, people could see what we were doing and that we were giving it a go and they jumped in to help. We were so grateful to not be alone on these projects because it's the loneliness that can become most overwhelming — that is part of why I created BuildHer Collective.

Skills are the other resource you need up your sleeve. We have built our own skill base — we have a great relationship with our trades, who are really mates. When I think back on the hours and help that some people have put into a project: Clint and Petro in particular, who have seen our deadline — generally a baby or Christmas or something in that ilk — and put in the time, starting early, finishing late or coming on a weekend to help on a job. Thank you Clint and thank you Petro! But honestly there is a team of people, too many to mention, who have bent over backwards to help us. And I have bent over backwards to help many others too as I know how hard it can be.

On our first projects we had mates who would give us mates rates. Sometimes my partner John would exchange services with them, or they would hang out on a weekend and help lift a wall or two. Everyone's lives have become busier now and property renovation is now our job. But in the beginning, when we were younger and had less grey hair, and fewer children and responsibilities, I have really fond memories of hanging out with friends, pouring a slab, cleaning a site or doing a task together. And it was fun!

No-one wants to be in the position where they are using people, but you do need to understand who you can rely on. Perhaps you are young and carefree and your mates are all trades. If you're lucky, you will have a family member who is a plumber, electrician, builder or joiner! Do you help each other? Do you know that you can rely on each other? Could you look at doing a project with someone similar to you if the thought of taking one on alone is too much?

It can be really uncomfortable to actually workshop where we are at, who is in our camp and what we could rely on — but don't let this be the reason why you don't look at building and renovating. Don't fear asking for help.

What types of projects interest you?

You can backfill many, many aspects of the building and renovating process. You can hire a designer, you can get help managing a project, you can even bring in some money. But you can't bring in the passion, the energy or the driving force.

This needs to come from you.

You will need to be the person who makes it happen. You will need to be the one who invests the time and energy, otherwise the people around you will not put in. Why would they?

We have learned that passion and energy are infectious: people love helping someone they can see going for it.

So, what are you passionate about? For me, it will always be the renovations! I love them: the unlocking potential, the starting with a base and turning it into something else. The art of taking something older and making it new again, of giving it a new lease on life. How incredibly fun and exciting is that! Renovation is the type of project that excites me — it makes me happy. A subdivision with eight townhouses doesn't bring me that same joy and so, since I can choose our projects, I choose the ones that bring me joy.

Creating your development plan

Ultimately, while reading through this book you will learn a whole pile of skills that you can apply to your project. I will equip you with tools to put in your toolbox that you can bring out when needed at a later date.

As you progress through the book, I want you to create your unique and actionable development plan. 'Development plan' is just a label for the plan that will be your reference point for your development journey — a document that maps your pathway towards your end goal!

The development plan you put together will need to consider the following:

— Access to cash

— Funding methods and borrowing capacity

— Time available to dedicate to the project

— Type of project

— Time frames of the project and expected returns.

And then, importantly, the plan will give you your pathway for how you will renovate or develop again and again to reach your end goal.

Please understand that this will be a working document. This is not a stagnant plan that you make, pop in a drawer and go forth and follow. Times have changed. The world is moving faster than ever before, and you can't know with 100 per cent certainty what the next project will look like until you have purchased it. So, your development plan needs to be flexible.

You will need to make a plan, then plan to replan the plan as the elements move and twist and you progress, working from the overarching goals back to the specific projects that will fulfil those goals.

By the time you've finished reading this book you should have an action plan that helps you understand how you can build and renovate your way to wealth.

Building your community

As we've already seen, community is key in the building game. No-one can do it alone. In my experience, when they try to, they inevitably get burnt out, exhausted and stuck! I know our lives are more disconnected than ever, but this game is so, so much more fun when you have a community supporting you.

There will be times on this journey, depending on the path you have taken, where you will second-guess yourself, where you will worry about the decisions you are making, where you will need a sounding board to make sure you are headed in the right direction.

I will show you how to build your networks of trusted professionals, but you will need and want friends. People who understand and are in it with you. There is a difference between having skin in the game and sitting on the sidelines. You will want to build your community of people who understand what it takes to make it through.

Why?

Because it's so hard to see the forest for the trees! There are so many small decisions to make. Once you get going you will be doing something that 99 per cent of people can't do so they won't understand you and will worry for you. And when they worry about you, they will want you to play it safe — and being safe is taking no risks. Yet, without risk there is no reward. And without the work that accompanies risk, there is no reward.

Pro tip

Find your people and gather them around you. People who understand and can guide you. People who get your 'why'.

If you have friends and family who get it, lean on them. If you don't, please come and join our DevelopHer Inner Circle. They could save you from making a hideous mistake or give you confirmation that you are actually on the right path.

At a minimum, have someone you can sound off, someone who will not get bored of the chats — ideally, someone who is on the same path as you.

I liken this to the newborn baby effect — the only person who really cares how often you got up during the night and how many wet and dirty nappies you changed is someone with a baby. As soon as they move on to baby's first steps, the game has changed and interest has moved on accordingly. Renovations are the same.

A friend of mine once said that there are no two topics more boring than renovations and babies, so given I had five children in 10 years and live in the world of renovations, I am sure I wasn't the best company for him!

Your secret sauce

Initially when you are renovating for profit or developing, you will want to learn the ropes, making decisions you can trust because they are tried and true. However, I would challenge you to find and embrace your secret sauce in the market you are working in.

What do I mean? Find the thing you love and are great at. What sets your projects apart from the rest? How is your view of the market and making money different from that of others and how does this allow you to operate in your own world?

For example, are you great at viewing older homes with an innate ability to unlock floorplans that others can't work with?

Do you have a unique and warm way of styling that the market is drawn to?

Do you work with finishes and materials that stand out in your market and make your homes more desirable?

While it is not essential to be different, it can help make your homes more attractive because they will sit uniquely in the market. Your product will look like *your* product and you can start to create demand around your homes. People will appreciate your unique approach — your special sauce — and they will be waiting for your homes to hit the market. This builds trust with the market for your brand and will help you build a relationship with that market over time.

You will work through this as you build your portfolio, as your creative flair develops and as you grow in confidence with every project you take on. I have my eye on a couple at the moment who build and renovate houses in Queensland. The first projects they completed were white on white. They were very mainstream and lovely. And in their latest renovations I've observed that they have doubled down on their craft and their style — and I'm here for it!

Case Study: Always moving and learning

I often talk about the journey and needing to love it – A LOT. The journey has been really great for our family and has allowed us to do things we wouldn't have thought possible. But each project has come with learnings and while overall the game is so fun, there have been moments where I might have been forgiven for giving up and not wanting to play anymore.

Here are some lessons from a few of our houses. As I have mentioned, there are always learnings — it is really important to grow, learn and reflect along the way:

House W

— Even though you love a home, other people may not share that joy. The layout needs to be perfect for them. When we sold our family home which had 6 bedrooms, three bathrooms, one living room, an outdoor study and a small courtyard garden, it was a complete surprise that other people didn't have so many children. The home was on a main road, and we loved the location. We renovated this home for ourselves and honestly there were so, so many lessons learnt.

— Find the ideal size home for your market and make it flexible.

— Remember, if you purchased at a discount because of a location, you might also sell at a discount for this same reason. It's a stepping stone.

— Sometimes holding on for the right amount is not the best solution. You need to cut your losses or take less profit, because moving forward will give you more gains overall.

— Releasing equity by staging works can allow you to build up the value over time and get started when you don't have all the cash available to renovate straight away.

(continued)

House M

— Trust your gut and build what you would want to live in! We have had so many forever homes that we have needed to sell for one reason or another. The best ones have been where we have put our heart and soul and really designed the space for family living.

— This project was the first time we really trusted our hearts and didn't just put a box on the back like all the other builders. Ironically, it was probably the biggest box we did. If you know something and the numbers support it, or if you have a product that is unique but will appeal to a large market in your area, then ultimately you are in control and can make the decisions.

— Think about your hero images from the beginning, these are the ones that will be used to showcase your home and draw purchasers.

— Sometimes pushing yourself can work out well, but remember you are still living while you are renovating and that means working, running a family and dealing with the highs and lows of life. Plan to have room for these things too.

— Staging works so you can live in the renovation saves a lot, but you might lack privacy. Our fridge was on the front porch as we completed the extension and one of our kind neighbours offered to buy it from us thinking we wanted to sell it.

House B

— Orientation matters, light is important, but you can overcome many of these issues with good design.

— We purchased this sweet little home which was south facing and boy it was dark. The wind blew the smoke from the chimney back inside the house, I was pregnant (again) and I hated living there. Working from home, having kids and living in a home with no space or light, and having a hypersensitive nose in a house filled with smoke did not bring me joy.

— Smaller renovations and extensions can be great. They are quicker and can still be transformative but they have a lot of appeal to a middle market.

— When you buy a home you can negotiate the terms including length of time, deposit amount and ability to move in before you settle.

House J

— It is possible to love a home in all its grandeur and potential unrenovated.

— Big old homes with big rooms can also be tricky as the size of the rooms and layout of the house are different to how we live now.

— If you aim to live in a home longer term while you go through the planning process then do what makes the most impact in the simplest way first.

— Sometimes when things get messy in the house, moving out for a short period of time to get a lot done is a good thing.

— Have fun with unfinished homes, when we renovated the master and ensuite, which was just one of the stages, we didn't want to install the carpet, as we wanted to do this all at the same time and there was still some messy work to complete. We painted the floor a lovely navy blue, which I would have never done if it was staying that way and I loved it!

— Make as much change in as few moves as possible. There is a lot to be said about keeping things in the same location and not moving every wall, try to work with what you have as much as possible.

(continued)

House N

— Sometimes you get angry neighbours. It is not about you it is about them and what they have going on in their life. Sometimes they need someone to be angry with because they are angry with life. Have grace and let it go.

— I spent a lot of money on some of the finishes in this house that I don't think anyone noticed or minded about. I debated timber or carpet upstairs and the form and flow of the home far outweighed the extras that I killed myself to make sure were the best of the best.

— Landscaping and design have a big impact, as do the views to existing trees and aspects.

House C

— Partnering with the right person is and can be amazing. On this home we partnered with my sister and I love working with her.

— Even bedrooms for children are best. Don't make potential purchasers have to pick a favourite child by making one room far better than the others, if possible.

— Hero moments are amazing, but a home needs to be highly functional and liveable too.

— You are buying a façade, a location and the aspect. When these are amazing it makes everything easier when you go to sell.

A quick recap

— Mindset is one of the biggest factors in overcoming your fear of taking action. It isn't easy, but if you can shift your mindset it is well worth it.

— Decide where you are heading and what this needs to look like by calculating your total asset base to estimate how much you will need to live comfortably.

— Understand what renovating, building or developing means to you. Then create your own pathway based on your values and passion, and make sure everything you do is aligned to this.

— Having capacity and supports in your system is paramount to getting a good result and not getting overwhelmed by the journey.

— Look at how you can bring your unique spice mix, or secret sauce, to the table, creating a blend that is unique to you, your skills and your abilities, and that you can use to leverage in the market.

— Create a development plan that will become the working document for mapping your pathway from where you are now to where you want to be.

The feasibility: your key to success

Let's get stuck into the nuts and bolts of what renovating for profit really is: doing a renovation where you spend less than you sell the property for. Simple, right?

Well it would be if everything was nicely laid out for you with exact costs, purchase prices and sale prices. This is not the case and while we can delve into all the areas that will help your renovations shine and that you can use to leverage, the first thing you need to understand is how to do a feasibility study, so you can work out what makes a profitable project.

Feasibility fundamentals

Feasibilities are a fundamental part of any project. But what are they exactly?

They are a big projected profit-and-loss statement. Renovating for profit is a business, after all so, as for all businesses, you need projected cash flows, profit and losses, assumptions... the works!

I have found the number-one issue with budding renovators is that they either don't do a feasibility or they don't complete it properly. They might do a back-of-envelope calculation, or believe the real estate agent's numbers: 'You buy for $X, add some stamp duty and costs, it'll cost you $200 000 to renovate — and Bob's your uncle, you've made money!'

The one thing that people miss is that they don't actually do a feasibility and work out all the costs. Yes, it can be overwhelming at first, but I'm here to help you.

We at BuildHer Collective have developed a template that we use as a bit of a checklist to make sure we're including all the numbers. Although the inputs and numbers will vary depending on the type of project you're looking to do, it's useful to start by using a template and then developing and adapting it to suit the complexity of each project.

After you've inputted the numbers, it isn't complicated — simple addition and subtraction is all that's needed. Likewise, it is great to start by using a template and then developing and adapting it to suit the complexity of your project. We have a template that you can download free from our website (www.buildhercollective.com .au/renovate) that includes the items listed in figure 2.1.

When you get good at doing feasibilities, filling out a spreadsheet like this one should only take a few minutes. But as with most things we do, the first attempt will be the hardest. You might never have engaged a geotechnical engineer so the process of working out how much to allow will be longer than if you have a reference point you can use. This is where knowledge and having a group of people around you who are doing this daily is really important. That way, you can leverage and build quickly.

Site and development information		
Site information	Address:	
	Block size:	
	Orientation:	
	Date:	
Planning restrictions	Planning overlays and restrictions:	
Proposed development description	What are you planning on doing to the property?	
Summary development costs		
Sale price (A)		
	Sale price (based on comparable case studies)	$
Acquisition costs (B)	Site purchase price	$
	All other acquisition costs	$
	Subtotal	**$**
Development costs (C)	Design and permits	$
	Demolition costs	$
	Planning, services and authorities	$
	Construction	$
	Landscaping	$
	Contingency	$
	Contribution fees	$
	Subtotal	**$**
Holding and sell costs (D)	Holding costs	$
	Sell costs	$
	Subtotal	**$**
Net profit		**$**

Figure 2.1: Sample feasibility template
Visit www.buildhercollective.com.au/bookdownloads to download this or any other template provided in this book.

The other thing to understand is that different types of builds have different costs, so you will need to make different allowances for different types of builds. Here's a pretty standard list of steps to follow:

Step 1: Create a scope of works.

Step 2: Work out what costings and information you will need to know.

Step 3: Understand how to gather this information accurately.

Step 4: Source your costings and update your feasibility.

Step 5: Check your assumptions and understand the potential profit.

If steps 1 to 5 check out and you proceed with the project, the final step will be to continually update your costs along the way so you get better and more accurate in future.

Accurate feasibilities are an art of scope and costs combined to deliver an outcome that makes a profit. It's no less involved than starting a business from scratch.

As you build up your knowledge and work through some projects you will also have the benefit of building a system for creating feasibilities. However, you do need to understand that there will always be movement and changes. You might understand how to do a renovation project easily, but then you have to tackle a knock-down rebuild, or you come across a scenario you haven't faced before — such as a site that needs the stormwater to be pumped to the legal point of discharge — and you'll feel a bit lost again. But you'll quickly learn to make allowances next time for a similar situation.

Before I jump to a few examples of different types of feasibility, as well as the information they might require and how you might go about calculating this information, let's look at some factors that affect all types of projects and how to approach them, as this will affect your pricing.

Location

Your choice of location can hugely impact your pricing. In any area, market forces will inevitably affect the cost of products and services — it's something that's commonly referred to as 'suburb tax'. For example, the people who service one area will charge a different amount for the same service as similar trades in a different area or location. Think about the difference you might find when comparing a quote for electrical works on a house located in a country town two hours away to one from the nearest satellite city; or a scope of works in the outer suburbs of a capital city to perhaps the same scope for a project located in the most affluent inner city suburb of that capital city. You would expect to see different pricing reflective of the location of your project.

Site conditions

All sites come with a set of conditions that you will inherit when you purchase it. These might include physical elements, such as a sloping block, which can be harder to build on and may require large amounts of earthworks. You may also need to use scaffolding and other safety measures.

Other site conditions include trees that you need to work around, buildings on your site, neighbouring properties and soil conditions such as rock or water table levels. Neighbouring properties is an interesting one, but one to consider. If you are building next to a home that has older style foundations or foundations on the boundary, you might need to consider whether your building works will, or have the potential to, undermine their property. An example of a complex situation might be a heritage home that is built on the boundary and founded on bluestone footings. If you were to build alongside these or in an area that might affect their structural integrity, there will be a cost attached. A typical engineering solution would be hit and miss blinding concrete along this footing and wall, which involves hand digging and staggering the pour in three different sequences to mitigate risk. The extra cost due to labour and materials, and potential for issues, is a consideration I would factor in when I purchase a property.

Site selection is really significant to the profitability of your project and some of these inherited costs can be big and costly.

Site access

Your method of getting access to the site to complete the work can also have a considerable impact on the costings due to complexity and labour costs — for example, for machines such as cranes that may be needed to move materials, or on the flip side, if there is limited access, which means you cannot get a machine onto the site. Such access issues will create higher costs due to material handling.

Other things to look out for include the location of powerlines, the size of the road you are building on and whether you need to allow for road closures or path of egress and how to move materials to the area where you want to build. For example, if you need to work on a site with no rear access you may need to man handle all the materials for an extension through a house. You'll also have to check that there is space for unloading materials. It could be that you need to block off a public space like a footpath or road, which would mean obtaining a permit from the council or may mean paying a fee to do so.

Each site has differing requirements depending on the site location, local area and infrastructure. Another example of increased cost is traffic management. For example, if you are building on a main road you may require traffic management to have trucks enter and exit the site during the build, whereas if you are building on a side street with little traffic there might not be any such requirements. We would recommend you think about the scope and how the builder or trades will be able to move on to and off the site with materials. In general terms, the harder and more complex this is, the more money it will cost.

Size of the project

The overall size of the project and staging of works throughout the build will need to be considered also. As a rule of thumb, a larger job where there is more flow of work for trades such as carpenters, plumbers and electricians will be more efficient than if the job is small and there are bits and pieces to do in different areas. To highlight this practically, if someone turns up to do a small job many times, it will cost more than having it all done at the one time. There are efficiencies to be found in the scale of a project and also the programming of these works.

Commonly I see people wanting to stage the work in terms of new build and renovation. They might want to live in the unrenovated part of the house while they build an extension, or renovate the inside of a house while waiting for planning permits or development approval. This can mean that the same trades need to come and go many more times, effectively sequencing the work from start to finish twice. This can add cost.

Complexity and quality of finish

What building method will you be using? Is there an implied level of quality and finish that needs to be taken into account? More complex projects require more labour hours to complete and a higher level of skill and craftmanship. This needs to be reflected in your scope of works and anticipated costings. Quality of finish might be in the craftmanship and labour, but it could also be in the materials required.

In your head you could be scoping for an expensive feature stone throughout, whereas I might be looking at a base-level laminate material. Either way, the scoping assumptions need to be incorporated into your costs and feasibility. Everyone has heard of champagne taste on a beer budget: if your budget is beer, understand this and base your feasibility on this level throughout both your costings and also your realised sale values. Do the same for champagne. If you exceed the expectation of the finish level with your beer budget, take that win. If you save money on your champagne budget, appreciate that also. Either way, preparing your feasibility with realistic, rational and achievable expectations will set you up for the win.

Standard vs custom specifications

Following on from the quality of finish, all costings effectively rely on two levers: labour and materials. These allow us to understand costings much better. Materials are just the cost of the physical material inputs, and labour is the time taken to turn your vision into reality.

In the case of materials, standard processes and components are less expensive than custom processes, which are built to order.

For example, if you're looking at installing cabinetry, you can buy modular, mass-produced, off-the-shelf cabinets, which will be more cost-effective due to the process and economies of scale than if you order customised, made-to-order shelving. Neither is right or wrong, but in the game of renovating for profit, you need to understand your return on investment. Will your selected materials have a positive or negative impact on your sale price?

Pro tip

One of my favourite ways to play this game is to use quality materials and a simple installation method. This means a lower labour cost with a great — though not hugely exorbitant — high-end result. It's fun to discover interesting and wonderful ways to use a product, but don't overlook the labour costs.

Project delivery

An important consideration when you're working out your feasibility is who you choose to work on your renovation. This will also have a knock-on effect on the length of time it will take you to complete the project.

If it's an owner-builder project (or done at mates rates) and you'll be doing the painting yourself, you might only be up for the material costs for paint. If you are you hiring a high-end builder, you'll need to align your budget with this method of building.

It will be impossible to work out your feasibility without considering your project delivery method. I have many conversations around budgets in relation to the level of professional services I'm looking at engaging. My belief is that every project is different and it is up to you to engage professionals that you think fit the outcomes you desire. You can renovate for profit as an owner-builder or with a high-end builder and still make money. You just need to know that this will work in your given market, which means the feasibility must support your building methods.

An example of this comes into play when choosing designers. At BuildHer Collective we use all levels of professionals. Depending on the project we might use a building designer, architect or an external interior designer, or we might do the design ourselves. When choosing a designer, we always look at the level of experience, the name that the professional carries, the designer's style of work and whether it is a good fit for the project.

A well-known interior designer might give you a much higher level of finish as an end-product; however, it may also cost a lot more to build because the intricacy of the build requires a lot of customisation to achieve your vision. In some cases, this will give you an amazing return on your investment and in others there is no budget to deliver the scope and make a profit. Assessing your market will be most important in this situation.

Other pricing aspects to consider

There are other factors that will have an impact on your pricing. You'll come across them as you get stuck into your project. At the beginning of a project I like to use a checklist like the one in figure 2.2 (overleaf) to record everything I expect will affect our pricing. Then, if any of my assumptions change I can come back to them and reassess the implications.

- [ ] **Location**
- [ ] **Site conditions**
- [ ] **Access issues**
- [ ] **Size of the project**
- [ ] **Complexity of the scope of works**
- [ ] **Assumption of quality**
- [ ] **Customisation**
- [ ] **Who is completing the work**
- [ ] **Level of the team being engaged**

Figure 2.2: Checklist of factors that affect renovation projects

Budgeting for a renovation

Okay, with a broad understanding of how the process will work in relation to costings, we'll now run through how to complete a feasibility for a renovation. You will need to make estimates based on the scope of works, materials and trades needed to be accurate. It can be difficult to estimate with a high-level square-metre rate here if you would like to create an accurate feasibility.

To get a base-level understanding, you might want to go in really high level with some allowances, but before you finalise your offer on a property and project you really need to work out an exact scope and put some budgets against it.

This will be a rolling budget, meaning it will update as you start to update the look and the feel of what you are doing. At this point, each finish and material should be assessed and calculated.

Steps for pricing items include:

Step 1: Mark up your scope of works on a plan.

Step 2: List each scope item, starting with the general items.

Step 3: Add a budget for each item on your scope.

Step 4: As you make selections and get quotes refine your scope, materials and budget.

Step 5: Add your budget to the feasibility worksheet.

Step 6: Adjust the contingency line item to reflect your level of knowledge and accuracy of the information you have available at this time.

Let's examine each stage of budgeting for a renovation more closely.

Step 1. Mark up your scope of works

Mark up a plan, loosely noting down the changes you want to make to each room (pen to paper works really nicely here). It's best if you can do this while you are walking around the property because you might pick up things that need to be fixed that you may not remember from a previous high-level walk-through. It's amazing how much the little items and costs start to add up as you unpick a site.

You may need to have a few goes at resolving the floorplan and scope of works. The more you change and move, the bigger the impact, so the name of the game is fewer moves for maximum return.

The High St renovation plan

High St was a renovation project that my family and I carried out.

We started with a high-level feasibility using some base amounts before drawing a rough plan of the work and discussing how we would achieve our vision.

When assessing the options, you are looking at the return on investment for the amount of work that is completed. We created a feasibility for three different scenarios, listing our indicative costs and working through this plan for each of the options.

When you are pricing or working out the cost there are a few different methods.

— Using price per m² for existing, areas that need a lot of work, and additional works. You might start with this type of budget.

— Using 'buckets' of money for each room. For example, $60k for the kitchen and $10k for the bedroom.

— Scoping and itemising the work, making allowances and then backfilling when you have more information.

— Using a quantity surveyor or builder to itemise and cost the project.

— A mix of all the above.

We will take you through the process I like to use which is scoping and itemising renovation works. This is way more accurate than allowing buckets or $/m² rates, but it does force you to consider what you will be doing early on, whereas the other methods allow more movement later in the process.

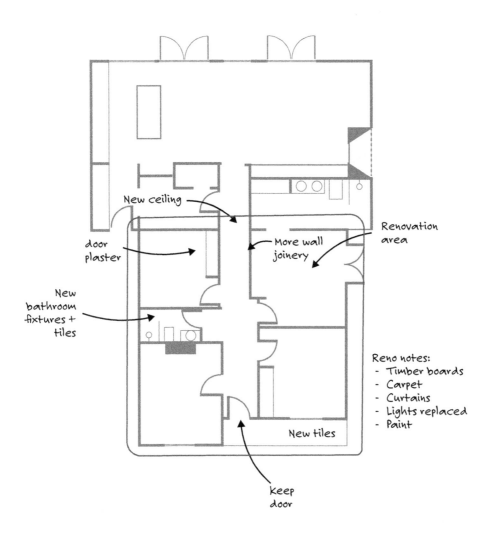

New ceiling

door plaster

New bathroom fixtures + tiles

More wall joinery

Renovation area

Reno notes:
- Timber boards
- Carpet
- Curtains
- Lights replaced
- Paint

New tiles

Keep door

Step 2. List your scope items

Once you have a broad plan that you are working to, narrow in on each scope item, thinking about who will complete the works and writing down any notes about the materials. This helps to define what material and labour you will need to complete the work. This will also help when it comes time to get a quote from a trade.

Table 2.1 Is an example of a list I used for one of my projects. At BuildHer Collective we already have a bank of suppliers, and we put them in the 'Materials/notes' column. You might not know who your suppliers will be at this point, so leave that column blank for now.

Table 2.1: An example of the scope of works items based on the High St Example. Note yours will be different

External Works Front Garden:	Who & Labor Notes	Material Notes / Supplier
Fix fence	Carpenter	
Pave walkway	Paver	
Regravel driveway	Carpenter	
Paint external house	Painter	
Tile front porch	Tiler	
New garden lighting	Electrician	
General Renovation Notes:		
New paint throughout	Painter	
Timber boards hallway	Carpenter	
New carpet	Carpet layer	
Replace all light fittings	Electrician	
New curtains to each bedroom	Curtain installer	
Bathroom General		
Demolish	Carpenter	
New flooring	Carpenter	
Rewire & fitoff bathroom	Electrician	
Replumb and fitoff bathroom	Plumber	

External Works Front Garden:	Who & Labor Notes	Material Notes / Supplier
Waterproofing	Waterproofer	
Tiling	Tiler	
Caulking	Caulker	
Replace window	Carpenter	
Bathroom Items		
Vanity	Carpenter	
Mirror	Carpenter	
Sink	Plumber	
Pop-up waste	Plumber	
Tapware (mixer and spout set)	Plumber	
Toilet (inbuilt cistern)	Plumber	
Inwall cistern	Plumber	
Push button/plate	Plumber	
Shower rose	Plumber	
Floor waste	Plumber	
Hooks x 2	Plumber	
Towel rail	Carpenter	
Floor tiles	Tiler	
Wall tiles	Tiler	
Shower screen	Shower screen installer	
Lights	Electrician	
Extraction fan	Electrician	
Window	Carpenter	
Entrance Hall		
Build in floor mat	Carpenter	
Replaster ceiling	Plasterer	
Move wall to master bedroom	Carpenter/Plasterer	
Replace door to master bedroom	Carpenter	
New lights x 2	Electrician	

(continued)

Table 2.1: An example of the scope of works items based on the High St Example. Note yours will be different (cont'd)

External Works Front Garden:	Who & Labor Notes	Material Notes / Supplier
Master Bedroom		
Remove window and replace with external doors	Carpenter	
Replaster ceiling and walls	Plasterer	
New joinery to wall	Joiner	
Create opening to extension	Carpenter	
Create bedhead	Carpenter	
New light	Electrician	
Bedroom 1		
New light	Electrician	
Bedroom 2		
New light	Electrician	
Fireplace surround	Carpenter	
Bedroom 3		
New light	Electrician	

Next you'll need a budget for each expense.

Step 3. Add a budget for each item

Depending on how decisive you are and how quickly you need to get the budget completed, you will either make allowances or select the exact items you will be using in your renovation.

The different items we selected and the budgets that we created for them are shown in table 2.2. You could use this as a base for your budget. The important thing here is to get a number or an allowance or some $ in the sheet for each item in your scope of works. This allows you to move quickly and actually get it done. As you get quotes and select items you will refine.

Table 2.2: An example of a scope with the budgets spreadsheet

External Works Front Garden:	Who & Labor Notes	Material Notes / Supplier	Number	Type	Allowance	Cost
Fix fence	Carpenter		1	Allowance	1	$100
Pave walkway	Paver		5	m²	$45	$225
Regravel driveway	Carpenter		1	Allowance	$500	$500
Paint external house	Painter		1	Allowance	$5000	$5000
Tile front porch	Tiler		10	m²	$45/m²	$500
New garden lighting	Electrician		1	Allowance	1	$500
					Subtotal:	$6825
General Renovation Notes:						
New paint throughout	Painter		1	Allowance	1	$5000
Timber boards hallway	Carpenter		14	m²	$60	$840
New carpet	Carpet layer		77	m²	$120	$9240
Replace all light fittings	Electrician		1	Allowance	$15000	$15000
New curtains to each bedroom	Curtain installer		4	Rooms	1200	$4800
					Subtotal:	$34880
Bathroom General						
Demolish	Carpenter		1	Allowance	1	$1500
New flooring	Carpenter		6	m²	$50	$300
Rewire & fitoff bathroom	Electrician		1	Allowance	$750	$900
Replumb and fitoff bathroom	Plumber		1	Allowance	1	$2000
Waterproofing	Waterproofer		1	Allowance	1	$2000
Tiling	Tiler		27	m²	$65	$1755
Caulking	Caulker		1	Allowance	$750	$750
Replace window	Carpenter		1	Allowance	1500	$1500
					Subtotal:	$10705

(continued)

Table 2.2: An example of a scope with the budgets spreadsheet *(cont'd)*

External Works Front Garden:	Who & Labor Notes	Material Notes / Supplier	Number	Type	Allow-ance	Cost
Bathroom Items						
Vanity	Carpenter		1	Item	1579	$1579
Mirror	Carpenter		1	Item	339	$339
Sink	Plumber		1	Item	237	$237
Pop-up waste	Plumber		1	Item	'36	$36
Tapware (mixer and spout set)	Plumber		1	Item	119	$119
Toilet (inbuilt cistern)	Plumber		1	Item	84	$84
Inwall cistern	Plumber		1	Item	1102	$1102
Push button/plate	Plumber		1	Item	892	$892
Shower rose	Plumber		1	Item	98	$98
Floor waste	Plumber		2	Item	21	$42
Hooks x 2	Plumber		1	Item	101	$101
Towel rail	Carpenter		1	Item	36	$36
Floor tiles	Tiler		6	m²	60	$360
Wall tiles	Tiler		21	m²	349	$7329
Shower screen	Shower screen installer		1	Allowance	750	$750
Lights	Electrician		3	Item	780	$2340
Extraction fan	Electrician		1	Item	259	$259
Window	Carpenter		1		$500	$500
					Subtotal:	$16203
Entrance Hall						
Build in floor mat	Carpenter		1	Item	158	$158
Replaster ceiling	Plasterer		1	Allowance	2200	$2200
Move wall to master bedroom	Carpenter/ Plasterer		1	Allowance	5000	$5000
Replace door to master bedroom	Carpenter		1	Allowance	1500	$1500
New lights x 2	Electrician		2	Allowance	215	$430
					Subtotal:	$9288

External Works Front Garden:	Who & Labor Notes	Material Notes / Supplier	Number	Type	Allow-ance	Cost
Master Bedroom						
Remove window and replace with external doors	Carpenter		1	Item	7500	$7500
Replaster ceiling and walls	Plasterer		54	m²	60	$3240
New joinery to wall	Joiner		3	Allowance	1400	$4200
Create opening to extension	Carpenter		1	Allowance	$2500	$2500
Create bedhead	Carpenter		1	Allowance	$3500	$3500
New light	Electrician		1	Item	207	$207
					Subtotal:	$21 147
Bedroom 1						
New light	Electrician		1	Item	345	$345
					Subtotal:	$345
Bedroom 2						
New light	Electrician		1	Item	345	$345
Fireplace surround	Carpenter		1	Item	650	$650
					Subtotal:	$995
Bedroom 3						
New light	Electrician		1	Item	345	$345
					Subtotal:	$345

Visit www.buildhercollective.com.au/bookdownloads to download this or any other template provided in this book.

With the materials, labour and costs sorted, it's time to fine-tune your scope and budget.

Step 4. Refine your scope, materials and budget

The budget you start with will not be the budget you finish with. I like to add a contingency on the amounts I have come up with, adjusting both the budget and the scope of works as I go and also the amount of contingency I am keeping available for the build.

You can see when you look at the numbers in this section that the costs associated with renovating the original part of the home are adding up as we make selections and allowances.

Next, we'll combine our budget with the feasibility worksheet.

Step 5. Add your renovation of the existing building budget to the feasibility worksheet

At this point you can go back and add the renovation numbers to the feasibility spreadsheet. I generally keep the contingency on the master feasibility, but you may wish to split them up.

There are many ways to run these numbers. The template I use is simple, making it super easy to run fast numbers, which is the key because you will often only have a very short window to work within (this can be the case if the project stacks up and you want to get started on it). No pressure!

That short window is why I like to use a template that is good for most renovation and small-scale development scenarios.

Step 6. Adjust the contingency line item

The contingency of a build or renovation is a moving item that will fluctuate throughout the build. In the beginning when you know less you will want a larger contingency. As you know more you will reduce your contingency to less as your project risk reduces. We would generally start with 20 per cent but if it is a smaller project and you really don't know what you are getting into, you may need more. If it is a bigger project and you have a lot of experience or you have started ratifying your costs, as in speaking to a builder, you may want to reduce this figure to 5 or 10 per cent.

This amount is the wiggle room you have in the build. Too tight and it will not be enough, but too generous and it may break your feasibility model and mean the project does not stack up.

Budgeting for an extension or new build

When we budget for new areas of work most of us are unable to accurately cost the structural elements of a build. First, we haven't had them designed yet, and second there are many ways to build and doing a quote can take days or weeks.

So, the method we use for this area is a little different and somewhat easier.

When budgeting, you will need to calculate the cost per square metre of the new build or new section and apply a rate that will enable you to build and finish the works.

The square-metre rate needs to take into account everything that will be included: footings, external walls, roof, fixtures and finishes. If there are any larger extra items such as a lift, specialty appliances or sometimes even an extra oven for the kitchen, you will want to separate them from the square-metre rate.

The way I calculate a square-metre area is by multiplying length by width. See the example that follows.

Working out a square-metre area

Referring to floor plan on the next page:

- Length = 12.6 m
- Width = 7.3 m
- So, if length × width = area (m²)
- Then 12.6 × 7.3 = approx. 92 m²

Next, we multiply this area by a rate per square metre to get an estimate of the total cost. In this case, our rate was $2200, so:

- 92 m² × $2200 = $202 400

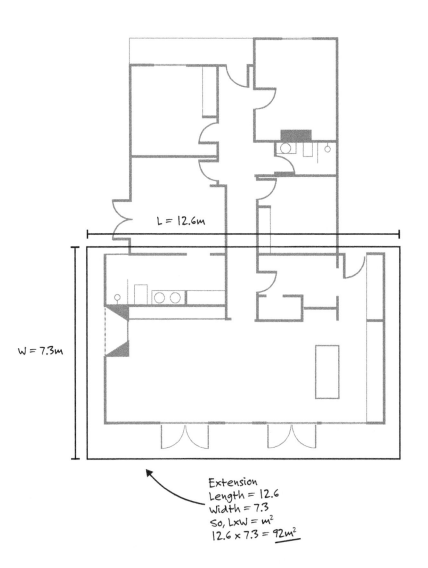

L = 12.6m

W = 7.3m

Extension
Length = 12.6
Width = 7.3
So, LxW = m²
12.6 x 7.3 = 92m²

Where am I getting the dollar per square metre rate?

The rate per square metre you allow will vary depending on the factors you have allowed for in your build. The substructure, site, access, finishes, complexity and who is building it all need to be taken into account.

In our case, we will be building the extension and an addition. Our renovation was small and on stumps and was designed efficiently using a lightweight construction method, which is quick and relatively easy as well as less expensive to install.

If we look to a square-metre reference guide such as the one prepared by BMT Quantity Surveyors (see their website), we can see that the range of construction costs runs from $1817/m² to $7444/m². This is a pretty wide range as it allows for residential builds and low-end standard builds to volume builds and high-end architectural builds.

You will need to determine your own pricing here, but coming up I will run through a few methods of ratifying costs.

Extras on top of the building costs

There will be additional costs that you'll have to add to your budget. Most of these relate to the design and permits. Which ones apply to you will depend on your site and your application. Table 2.3 lists some of the consultants and services you're likely to require depending on your project. Who you need to engage will depend heavily on the type of project and what you are hoping to achieve.

You now have a checklist that you can use to make sure you include all the costs — a handy tool for your renovation toolbox.

Going back to our High St family project, you can see all the relevant numbers inputted into the spreadsheet on page 55. Note that we already owned this property so we haven't included stamp duty into the value of the property.

Table 2.3: Design and permit costs associated with an extension or new build

Consultants	Estimate of cost
Architect/design	
Building surveyor	
Civil engineer	
Energy report	
Interior designer	
Land surveyor	
Landscape architect	
Planning consultant	
Soil investigation report	
Structural engineer	
Traffic consultant	
Demolition and related costs	
Arborist report	
Asbestos	
Demolition	
Tree removal permits	
Planning, services and authorities	
Asset protection	
Crossover	
Electrical, incl. pits	
Gas connection	
NBN	
Sewer points incl. contributions	
Stormwater incl. retention	
Stormwater legal point of discharge application	
Subdivision	
Water tapping	
Landscaping	
Fencing incl. front fence	
Lawn and plants	
Paving, paths, seats, mailbox	
Pools incl. pool fencing	

(continued)

Table 2.3: Design and permit costs associated with an extension or new build (cont'd)

Consultants	Estimate of cost
Contribution fees	
Open space	
Levies (subdivision/planning)	
Holding costs	
Bank package fees	
Council rates	
Interest on construction loan	
Interest on current mortgage	
Land tax	
Selling costs	
Agent's fees	
Legals	
Marketing	
Mortgage discharge fee	
Property styling	

Visit www.buildhercollectivecom.au/bookdownloads to download this or any other template provided in this book.

The High St renovation options

We completed the feasibility numbers three times with different options and scope of works. This is a great way to put some numbers around making a decision, you can see in the first option we would just sell the property. The second option was to do an internal renovation and the final option was to renovate the existing house and to build an extension. This is a great way to make decisions. So often I see people show me projects where they have decided to build a big extension because they love that project, but it can be better and easier to just renovate internally. It really depends on the numbers.

OPTION 1 – Keep it as-is

Description of works: Do nothing but clean and no styling.

Assumptions: Number based on a comparable sale of $1 000 000.

PROS	CONS
Really quick.	Currently it looks horrible and smells appalling.
Only cleaning – no reno fees.	Would be sold to someone who wanted to renovate so would generally not produce a good outcome.
Leanest on holding costs.	No appeal to the purchaser, purely numbers game.

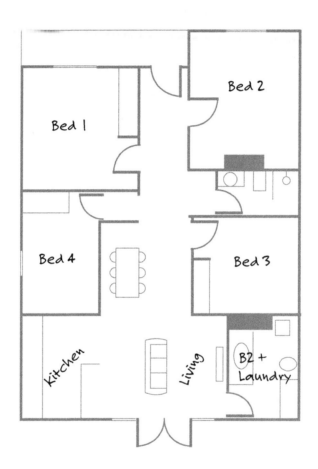

Site and development information		
Site information	**Address:**	
	Block size:	
	Orientation:	
	Date:	
Planning restrictions	Planning overlays and restrictions:	
Proposed development description	What are you planning on doing to the property?	
Summary development costs		
Sale price (A)		
	Sale price (based on comparable case studies)	$1 000 000
Acquisition costs (B)	Site purchase price	$1 000 000
	All other acquisition costs	$0
	Subtotal	**$1 000 000**
Development costs (C)	Design and permits	$0
	Demolition costs	$0
	Planning, services and authorities	$0
	Construction	$10 000
	Landscaping	$3000
	Contingency	$0
	Contribution fees	$0
	Subtotal	**$13 000**
Holding and sell costs (D)	Holding costs	$17 500
	Sell costs	$27 500
	Subtotal	**$44 000**
Net profit		**$-58 000**

OPTION 2 – Renovate within the existing footprint

Description of works: Due to the state of the home, which is not useable or saleable, we would need to replace the bathroom, laundry and kitchen. A deck or stairs would need to be built to the backyard, the garden cleaned up, the house repainted.

Assumptions: Site worth $1 m. Based on comparable sale of $1 220 000.

PROS	CONS
Can be completed quickly: 2/3 months.	Not the ideal living arrangement.
Minimal spend on renovation.	Might be hard to sell.
Minimal spend on holding costs.	Need to do a lot of the work that we would do on a full-scale renovation, but without the impact.
Limited spend on consultants.	

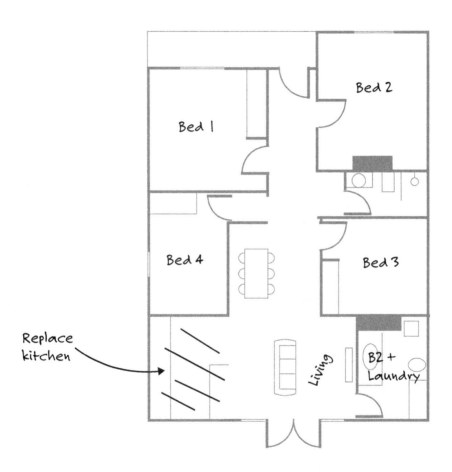

Site and development information		
Site information	**Address:**	
	Block size:	
	Orientation:	
	Date:	
Planning restrictions	Planning overlays and restrictions:	
Proposed development description	What are you planning on doing to the property?	
Summary development costs		
Sale price (A)		
	Sale price (based on comparable case studies)	$1 220 000
Acquisition costs (B)	Site purchase price	$1 000 000
	All other acquisition costs	$0
	Subtotal	**$1 000 000**
Development costs (C)	Design and permits	$0
	Demolition costs	$0
	Planning, services and authorities	$0
	Construction	$100 000
	Landscaping	$15 000
	Contingency	$10 000
	Contribution fees	$0
	Subtotal	**$125 000**
Holding and sell costs (D)	Holding costs	$35 000
	Sell costs	$38 500
	Subtotal	**$73 500**
Net profit		**$21 000**

OPTION 3 – Renovate and extend

Description of works: Leave plaster, walls, reconfigure, make pretty and add an extension to the rear of the property. Build a new deck and landscape.

Assumptions: Site worth $1 m. Based on Sale Comparable: $1700 000.

PROS	CONS
Possibility of a better return due to better configuration of the house.	We have to spend more money up front.
Easier to sell a finished house in this market.	Longer time frame and can't get money until finished.
I like the project and want to do it – more aligned with values.	More potential for costs to blow out.
A lot of the work would need to be done in the above plan.	More time in design and planning.

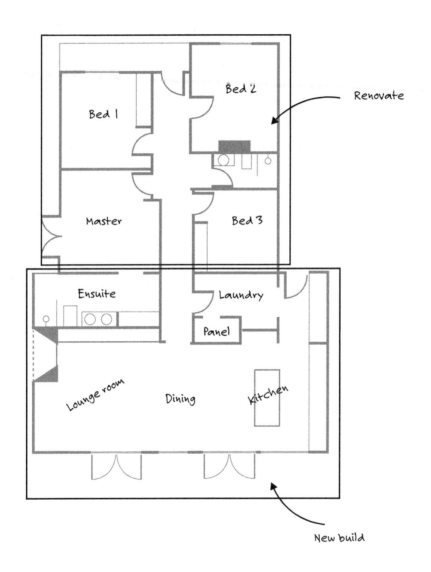

Renovate

Bed 1

Bed 2

Master

Bed 3

Ensuite

Laundry

Panel

Lounge room

Dining

Kitchen

New build

Site and development information		
Site information	**Address:**	
	Block size:	
	Orientation:	
	Date:	
Planning restrictions	Planning overlays and restrictions:	
Proposed development description	What are you planning on doing to the property?	
Summary development costs		
Sale price (A)		
	Sale price (based on comparable case studies)	$1 700 000
Acquisition costs (B)	Site purchase price	$1 000 000
	All other acquisition costs	$0
	Subtotal	**$1 000 000**
Development costs (C)	Design and permits	$33 850
	Demolition costs	$15 000
	Planning, services and authorities	$0
	Construction	$250 000
	Landscaping	$50 000
	Contingency	$30 000
	Contribution fees	$0
	Subtotal	**$378 850**
Holding and sell costs (D)	Holding costs	$70 000
	Sell costs	$27 500
	Subtotal	**$97 500**
Net profit		**$223 650**

Ultimately, you will need to have knowledge of your project and site and what costs and fees are going to be appropriate to bring you your desired outcome. That's what the next section is about.

Resources for getting your numbers right

The key to getting your numbers right is understanding what needs to go in your feasibility and making sure you input accurate numbers. But how exactly does that work?

I will go back to the idea that the price or cost of anything is fluid. It is based on labour and materials, and finding someone who is willing to complete the work as well as understanding how much they will charge for completing it.

Hmmmm, so what does that mean for you when you are working out costs?

Over time you will build up a bank of consultants you can trust and get to know how much they charge. You will acquire a honed system and a circle of people you can work with, all of which will make these assumptions easier to manage. You will also learn to assess a site — assessing the requirements will become second nature. But for now, I'm here to guide you.

Calculating your numbers accurately is an art: one that will require common sense and a good understanding of the project, and most likely a heap of research. You will need to make assumptions and then set about ratifying your numbers to ensure accuracy.

You will ratify your numbers by:

— referring to price guides like Cordell's or Rawlinson's and other quantity surveying reports

— speaking to builders in the area

— speaking to other people building in the area

— researching and understanding your product and material selections

— speaking to real estate agents

— using insurance calculators (google 'Cordell calculator').

The biggest problem we face is that what one person can build for another cannot. The build price is a compilation of many trades as well as the systems and overheads that the builder will use to run the project, plus their profit margin.

For one dual occupancy project I took on, the highest and lowest concreting quotes were $50 000 apart and ranged from $100 000 to $150 000. On any one project you have many to hundreds of quotes, and the decisions on who you engage and the scope of their work will form the basis of the price.

As far as labour goes, you might find one person happy to work for $30 per hour and another who won't accept less than $150 per hour for the same job. But they will work at different speeds and will purchase different materials, which they will charge to the project. This can lead to some vastly different quotes for the same aspect of the build.

What does this teach us?

We need to understand not just the numbers, but the 'how' it will be built behind the numbers and if we are hiring trades directly then obtaining multiple quotes is always a good idea.

In our BuildHer Collective community we provide a forum where people can submit their feasibilities and we help them work through their assumptions and how to ratify the numbers, including delving into whether they sound right or not.

Remember, there is no right or wrong here — however, there is a process to follow to ensure accuracy. And it is worth putting this time in upfront. It is worth the time and effort as ultimately this will be the difference between a successful project and one that doesn't have the required funds.

The next section will give you an example of this process.

Quantifying the cost

As you've seen, when we assess the cost of building we are essentially dealing with two things: labour (or time) and materials. How you combine these two key aspects will determine the cost.

Let me explain this a little more for you. Labour is the input of time and how much someone's time costs in dollars, and the materials are the physical inputs.

Every decision you make on your renovation will have a consequence in costs. By using time and materials we can calculate any aspect of the build. Learning the basics of building is the first step towards quantifying the costs.

Planning a bathroom reno

To help get your head around how decisions change and affect the cost, let's keep working through part of the bathroom renovation presented in table 2.1 (see page 40). We will focus on the tiling by working through our budget for tiling the bathroom floor and walls.

The steps involved are:

1. Draw a floorplan of the bathroom to scale.
2. Mark all fixtures and fittings to scale.
3. Draw an elevation of the room.
4. Add bathroom fixtures, considering details and standards.
5. Select and document the materials and fixtures.
6. Prepare a materials costing schedule.

Step 1. Draw a floorplan

Drawing the floorplan of your bathroom to scale will enable you to clearly see how it will look. This, in turn, will help you to manipulate the exact quantities of materials you need. I like to use grid paper to make it really easy to draw your floorplans (see figure 2.3).

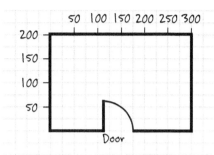

Figure 2.3: Example of the bathroom drawn to scale

1. Draw your floorplan on the grid by marking out the length and width of the bathroom.

2. Add doors and windows in place to ensure you have a good flow through the space.

3. Consider the thickness of your walls and ensure your line weights match.

Step 2. Mark all fixtures and fittings to scale

There are two parts to this step (see figure 2.4):

— Use the dimensions of the room on your grid paper to loosely mark out the room onto tracing paper to use as a template later.

— Draw in, or trace over, the bathroom fixtures in the room to scale — toilet, vanity/ies, shower and bath — checking dimensions.

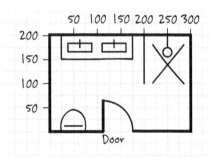

Figure 2.4: Example of the bathroom with fixtures and fittings drawn on the floorplan

Here's a dimensions cheat sheet to help you along.

Shower width	900–1200 mm
Toilet space	900–1200 mm
Vanity depth	450–500 mm
Vanity width	900–1800 mm
Bath length	1500–1900 mm
Bath width	800 mm
Freestanding clearance	100 mm
Shower opening	750 mm min.
Screen length	900 mm min.
Shower shelf	90–200 mm

Step 3. Draw each wall elevation of your room

The elevation is the length of the wall multiplied by the ceiling height. Ceiling heights vary but will generally sit between 2400 and 3000 mm. Make sure you draw all four wall elevations (see figure 2.5).

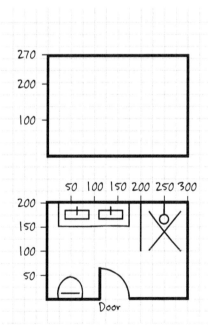

Figure 2.5: An example of the wall elevation with a ceiling of 2.7m

Step 4. Draw bathroom fixtures onto the wall elevation

This is the important bit. While it may take a while to perfect the skill of doing this, when you learn how to draw an elevation you are learning not only how to communicate what will be happening in the room in detail, but also how to resolve issues and troubleshoot before you build the room. It is so much cheaper to figure out the solution on paper than by building and rebuilding!

An easy way to do this is to project the lines up (see figure 2.6). Then draw everything you would see in front of you as if you were looking at the wall. Use the tracing paper template to trace the bathroom fixtures to scale, or draw them freehand using standard dimensions.

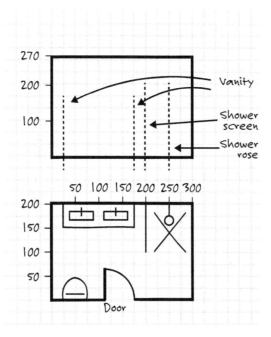

Figure 2.6: An example of how you can map the fixtures and finishes from the floor to the wall easily

As you work through this elevation, you will be making many decisions along the way. All of these decisions have an implication when it comes to cost: it may be time or materials. An example of the materials cost might be whether to choose an expensive or a cost-effective tap. An example of labour might be moving the toilet to where you have an existing slab, or installing tiles that are a thick, natural stone and hard to cut and lay.

These are the fixtures you will need to draw into your elevation, and some of the decisions you'll have to make along the way:

— Under-mount or vanity-mounted sink? This will determine the vanity height.

— Vanity to be wall hung or on the floor?

— Countertop thickness.

— Finger pull or handles to open cabinets? Drawers or cupboards?

— How will the shower open?

— Toilet.

— Decide on toilet roll holder height and location.

— Add in a niche or ledge if required and if size allows for it.

— Add a mirror.

— Add taps: wall mounted, hob mounted, mixer?

— Add shower: twin set or rain head?

— Add hooks and towel rails.

— Decide on and add joinery materials, countertop, tiles. Decide on locations, heights and thicknesses.

— Think about and add lighting and power points where you think they should go.

— Make sure you note the materials on your elevation by using a code — for example, 'T01' for 'tiles type 1'.

— Add notations so you can remember what you were thinking.

Figure 2.7 shows what this would look like with the fixtures drawn to scale.

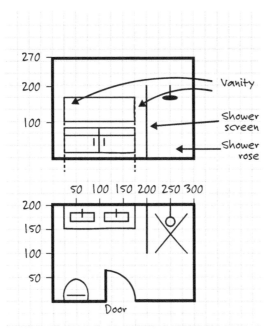

Figure 2.7: An example of how the elevation will look with the fixtures drawn on to scale

Here's another helpful dimensions cheat sheet.

Shower head height	2000 mm
Shower screen height	2100–2400 mm
Vanity height	900 mm
Bath height	450 mm
Tap height above sink	150 mm
Bench thickness	20–100 mm
Mixer height	750 mm
Toilet roll holder width	700 mm
Tile thicknesses	9–20 mm

Step 5. Select and document the materials and fixtures

It's time to start choosing your materials. This is where design and creativity come into play.

Every face of your drawing needs to be marked up with the materials required. You'll need to include:

— floor tiles

— wall tiles

— tapware material

— mirror details

— joinery materials

— stone selections

— handles.

As you think about your design, add materials to the surfaces in your mind. Then play with the physical samples to create a materials board like the one in figure 2.8.

Image	Code	Location	Supplier	Colour	Finish

Figure 2.8: Materials board

Pro tips

As you create a materials board, give each item a code and, importantly, note the cost per square metre or cost per item.

Take a photo of the materials so you can see how they will look together and start to visualise the space you're renovating.

Step 6. Prepare a materials costing schedule

Now you have done this you can populate your materials costing schedule (see figure 2.9 for an example). I like to do this in an Excel spreadsheet as it gives me the flexibility to change items and adjust my design and costs easily.

Image	Supplier name	Material location	Number/m²	$/m² or allow	Cost

Figure 2.9: Materials costing schedule
Visit www.buildhercollective.com.au/bookdownloads to download this or any other template provided in this book.

There are a few measurement standards and terms to be aware of (*reminder:* m² = length × width).

tiles	$/m²
tiler	$/m²
stone	$/m² or number of slabs
joinery	allowance/quote
mirrors	itom
tapwares	item
paint	allowance
handles	item
lights	item
shower screen	item

Tiling the bathroom

Now for the critical analysis work ...

We will work though the tiling aspect of the bathroom.

Let's say when you were planning the bathroom reno you were happy to use some pretty standard tiles that cost $60/m² and the tiler was charging you $80/m² to install them.

Here are the measurements for the bathroom tiles. You will be tiling the floor and the walls from floor to ceiling (2.7 m height) with 'average' tiles. The areas to be covered are:

floor	2.0 × 3.0	6.0 m²
wall a	3.0 × 2.7	8.1 m²
wall b	2.0 × 2.7	5.4 m²
wall c	3.0 × 2.7	8.1 m²
wall d	2.0 × 2.7	5.4 m²

So, the area to be covered by tiles = 33 m²

Add 10 per cent wastage = 3.3 m²

Total area = 36.3 m²

You'll find the total cost of purchasing the tiles and the installation cost in table 2.4.

Table 2.4: Changing the cost of the tiles (@ $60/m²) and installation (@ $80/m²)

Bathroom tile costing	Length	Width	m²	
Floor	2.00	3.00	6.00	
Wall a	3.00	2.70	8.10	
Wall b	2.00	2.70	5.40	
Wall c	3.00	2.70	8.10	
Wall d	2.00	2.70	5.40	
		Subtotal	33.00	
Total tile area:			33.00	
Wastage (10%):			3.30	
Total to order:			36.30	
	$		m²	
Amount per m²: tiles:	$60	×	36.30	$2178.00
Amount per m²: installation:	$80	×	36.30	$2904.00
	$140			$5082.00

Now let's say you found some tiles that are a little bit fancier than the average ones and they cost $150/m². They are smaller and need to be individually installed, which take the tiler longer so the installation charge will be $120/m².

To work out how many tiles you will need, you need to know the area you are tiling and the best way to do this is, once again, to draw an elevation of the bathroom walls.

Looking at table 2.5 (overleaf), you can see that adjusting the total amount of tiles needed you can manipulate the cost — you are actually able to justify using the more expensive tile choice and get pretty close to the same cost as for the more average tiles.

Table 2.5: Changing the cost of the tiles ($150/m²) and installation ($120/m²)

Bathroom tile costing	Length	Width	m²	
Bathroom tile costing	Length	Width	m²	
Floor	2.00	3.00	6.00	
Wall a	3.00	2.70	8.10	
Wall b	2.00	2.70	5.40	
Wall c	3.00	2.70	8.10	
Wall d	2.00	2.70	5.40	
		Subtotal	33.00	
Total tiles:	33.00			
Wastage (10%):	3.30			
Total tiles to order:	36.30			
	$		m²	
Amount per m² tiles:	$150	×	36.30	$5445.00
Amount per m² installation:	$120	×	36.30	$4356.00
	$270			$9801.00

Another option would be to manipulate the extent of tiles. At the moment we are tiling floor to ceiling on each of the four walls, but we can also change where we tile and the height at which we tile in order to manipulate the costs. In Figure 2.10 you can see the wall is tiled to 2.7m, but in Figure 2.11 the wall is only tiled to 2.1m. This is something I like to do both because it looks great and it reduces the extent of the tiles and tiling and therefore minimises cost.

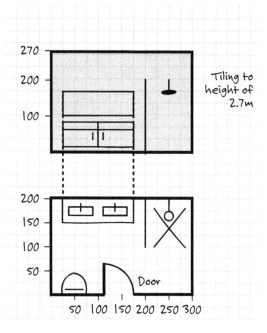

Figure 2.10: An example of the extent of tiling when tiling to 2.1m high

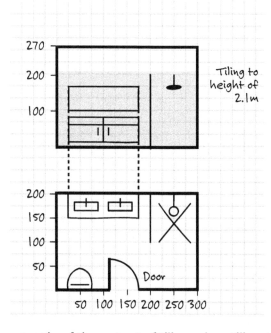

Figure 2.11: An example of the extent of tiling when tiling to 2.7m high

Table 2.6 shows the costing when the extent of the tiling has reduced from 2.7m high to 2.1m high.

Table 2.6: Changing the quantity of the tiles

Changing the quantity of the tiles					
Bathroom tile costing	Length	Width	m²		
Floor	2.00	3.00	6.00		
Wall a	3.00	2.10	6.30		
Wall b	2.00	2.10	4.20		
Wall c	1.00	2.10	2.10		
Wall d	0.00	2.10	0.00		
		Subtotal	18.60		
Total tiles:	18.60				
Wastage (10%):	1.86				
Total to order:	20.46				
	$		m²		
Amount per m² tiles:	$150	×	20.46	$3069.00	
Amount per m² installation:	$120	×	20.46	$2455.20	
	$270			$5524.20	

You may look at this and think, 'Eek! That's too much!' when it comes to renovating for profit, but when I look at this I think about how much control we have. The costs, which, as we know, are just labour and materials, are completely within our control! Remember, we set the budget and we have to justify the project we are putting together and, from an emotive perspective, visualise getting a return on our investments.

The cost of the project is in essence a selection of these types of calculations about what will or won't be required and how much the materials and labour will cost along the way.

The cost of action vs inaction

Starting your property renovation or development journey will possibly be daunting — especially financially. The end goal will excite you, but making the actual decision to go for it can be scary.

It's okay. You're not alone, and I hope that with the help of this book, you will learn how to leverage your cash, calculate the return on investment and manage all the variables in order to make sound financial decisions based on numbers rather than emotions. You will be investing with an expected return — not just taking a punt and hoping it works out. However, to do this you need to take action.

The importance of action

It can be tempting to go all in on something like a renovation with back-of-envelope numbers and hopes. Putting actual energy into calculating the return and numbers upfront can be a little overwhelming. But it's essential.

Think of it this way:

— If you were doing this as a job and you had to present the best option and justify this to your boss, how many feasibilities would you complete?

— If you completed one feasibility rigorously, understanding and calculating each of the inputs — including the scope of works and verifying costs — how confident would you be to do another? How long would you expect the first feasibility to take? (We all know it's always the first one that's the hardest!) How long would you expect the 100th to take?

- After you've completed, say, 10 feasibilities, do you think you would start to see patterns in what is working well and what is not?

- How many feasibilities do you think it would be reasonable to do before you learn to recognise a project that is an outlier and one that can give you bigger returns than the others?

I can do a feasibility in a few minutes. If it stacks up, I would then re-look at the opportunity and think about how I might be able to verify and I'd then spend more time on how I would proceed — in particular whether it is actually realistic.

I'd spend time looking more at the scope of the project and how to achieve the result in as few moves as possible rather than any other aspect of the build. After the initial numbers are run, it is easy to decide whether it is worth the time and effort to delve further into the build. When I am actually working on a project, this is one of the fun bits: what can I do and how do I create the best home I can within the budget and working with the conditions on-site?

The first feasibility you run might take you 10 hours to get accurate, but the next would probably only take two and the third might take only one hour.

I find that people wait until they have the money to buy the property before doing a feasibility. And then, once they do, they feel like they don't have time to do the work as they need to buy *now*... which means they never actually do the work before jumping all in on a potential project.

Can you see how this becomes an issue that doesn't help you learn or put you in the best position to purchase well? It's better to take action first.

The hidden cost of time

Now, we all know it is easier to do nothing and just keep the status quo. But the reality is that you picked up this book and started reading because you're looking to become a renovator.

Time is going to march by no matter what action you do or don't take. Time has a cost. It has value in terms of what your money could do for you over time if it were working for you.

For starters, let's consider the cost of staying where you are:

— *Lost potential:* Every day you delay your property renovation or development journey, you miss out on the potential for growth and prosperity. The longer you wait, the harder it becomes to catch up. What if you had got into the property market 5 years ago? Where would you be now? (Can I ask that question enough?)

— *Opportunity cost:* This is about whether you have a project in play or not. Is the money you're not investing in your property development working for you elsewhere? For example, if your money is making 4 per cent in a fixed rate interest account, then taking this money out of action to purchase a property would mean that the cost of that money is 4 per cent.

Leveraging is the key to success and how you can build wealth. Every dollar you can have working for you to increase your property's value and your wealth is a cost for which you should see a return on investment (ROI). So often I see people choose options that make them feel better but don't provide a lot of growth.

I only know property — it is my investment vehicle, and obviously one you are interested in. It is one where we see great returns through renovating for profit in the short term. But you need to understand this is not a passive strategy. You are trading time for money with the strategy that by doing this you will be able to bump up the value of your cash significantly in return for that time.

What we want to ascertain here is the return on our money over the period of time we have it working for us.

Here is a hypothetical for you.

Townhouse or reno?

You have $500 000 in the bank earning 4 per cent per year and you'd like a better return on your money.

You're trying to decide whether to do a townhouse project or a renovation.

— *Option 1:* the townhouse project would take two years and has an expected return of $400 000.

— *Option 2:* the renovation would take six months and has an expected $150 000 return.

Here's how I would run this calculation (to keep things simple, I've assumed interest is accruing yearly, not daily).

Cash in the bank: $500 000 @ 4 per cent gives me a return of $20 000 per year.

Option 1: townhouse project = $400 000 / 2 = $200 000 per year

$200 000 / $500 000 = 40 per cent return on investment per year.

Option 2: renovation project = $150 000 for 6 months

$150 000 / $500 000 = 30 per cent for 6 months = 60 per cent return for a year if you do two projects and all things being equal.

Of course, it's not just a numbers decision. You also have to make assumptions and weigh up the pros and cons.

Here's how you might look at the pros and cons. They are partially numbers based and partially values based.

Option 1—townhouse project:

- — *Pro:* has a time component that would allow you to hire a builder and work at your full-time job. It could be an easy juggle and would be controllable from this perspective.

- — *Pro:* for the one lot of time input the consistency of this return is 40 per cent over 2 years.

- — *Con:* If the project gets held up in planning and takes an additional year, the returns would change significantly to:

    - – $400 000 / 3 years = $133 000 per year.

    - – $133 000 / $500 000 = 26.6 per cent return.

- — *Con:* as the project runs over 2 years there are probably more risk associated with the variables, the market and costs associated with the build.

Option 2—renovation project:

- — *Pro:* has a good return for 12 months of work.

- — *Pro:* you can have pretty good confidence in the market and control of the inputs over this amount of time.

- — *Pro:* this is a fun, hands-on project.

- — *Con:* there is a lot of time input in a short amount of time and if you wanted to sustain this return you would need to have another project lined up to start when you finish.

The cost-of-money-over-time-with-effort equation is a good way of looking at the project a little bit more impartially. Ultimately, it doesn't matter if it is property or stocks — or something else — your money just needs to be at work.

Now, of course there is risk and of course things can turn out better or worse, but the main thing you want to look at in your projections is how your proposed project might come to fruition if you take one action over another. When you start seeing opportunity you will find you are more limited by your resources, time, energy and cash reserves than you are by fear. This means that when you commit you need to know with a degree of certainty that this is the right thing for you to do.

Our most important asset: time

Freedom is so high on our radar … for us any move we make has to also consider our family! And while I don't agree with changing strategy all the time, I do believe you should follow your passion. Just because you have always done something a particular way, doesn't mean you can't change it up. For example, just because you know how to work for someone doesn't mean you should only do that. Have you sat down recently and looked at how this game of life could be if you were brave enough to get started, if you were brave enough to start doing the things you wanted to do, like renovating? Can you dare to dream big and instead of thinking about all the reasons why you can't, change the conversation to how you can?

There is a cost-and-reward ratio that will always be at play. If you do enough projects, you are bound to get better at working this out, while also occasionally making a mistake or investment that doesn't perform as well as the others. I use property renovation and development to create wealth, so if I am not doing this and actively playing the game, then the cost of my inaction will grow.

While you're taking time waiting for the right time, life is continually getting more expensive. I have never known a time when we were not complaining that things cost too much. The hurdles don't get easier — they get harder to jump and it can almost always feel like you have missed the boat and you needed to jump into starting your renovation journey 5 years ago. I think I have been hearing people say that to me for over 10 years now. I know it is hard now, but the sooner you find a way, the better. That might mean pairing up with a sibling like I did all that time ago to buy our first renovator. You may have the loveliest sister ever, like me — thanks Caitlin — or you may have to move slightly further afield and find a different opportunity. There are many ways to play if you are willing to put the time and effort into making a change.

You can look at this from the point of view of what you might actually accomplish in 5 years, how you might be able to push forward, how you might be able to get a project — or two or three — under your belt. Perhaps even more, depending at how fast you move. My journey has felt both tediously slow at some points and super quick at others. Have a think about what you could be giving up by talking and not acting on your dreams.

Decisions and values

The thing that keeps renovating and building for profit interesting and dynamic, as I keep mentioning, is that there is no hard and fast right and wrong. Just as soon as I have seen a formula work a few times, I have seen someone else break it by pushing the boundaries in a different way, in a different market, and have outstanding success. I have heard many questions from people around rules: can't we buy, spend 30 per cent on a renovation and sell. Well no, I understand why you want this but it simply does not work in all cases and there is no rule that does.

So now that you have let go of wanting rules to follow and an exact formula that means you will be painting by numbers, we can actually look at what you need to focus on. That is, you need to spend enough to make a wonderful and beautiful product that the market will fight over but not so much that you are jeopardising or eating into your profit by providing anything that's not needed.

I can almost hear you mutter, 'Great, thanks for that — easier said than done'. Yes, it is, but this is the magic. This is the bit that takes your project from just another project to a work of art — one where you get to create something unique and special and bring your vision to the world.

Fun, right?

Yes! It is super fun — so, so much fun.

There is no room for complacency. This is a game that needs thought and action alongside it. You will need to really get clear on property in your market: on what is valued and what is not.

I'll give you an example that one of our DevelopHers and I were debating... In her market, split systems are the norm. People have them on the wall and they are not seen as a dealbreaker — in fact, they are not even noticed. However, in my market — one that is a little more sensitive to the aesthetic and, in fairness, a more expensive market — I would never be able to do this without jeopardising the end sale price. My market will look at that and think I cut corners throughout the whole build.

What does this mean? You get to delve into the world of decisions and ROI. And when you are looking at ROI, this is a subjective game that you can debate wholeheartedly.

Here's a quick guide to some decisions you might have to make:

— Quality of finish on the kitchen: do you need stone?

— 'To pool or not to pool': that is always the question!

— Do you need a security system?

— Do you need to build in speakers and an entertainment system?

— Does the kitchen need to have a butlers pantry?

— Does the main bedroom need to have a walk-in robe, or could this be built-ins?

— Do you need a garage or carport; double or single?

— Do you need expensive tiles or can you use cheaper ones cleverly?

- How much landscaping do you need to do?
- Does the market pay more for timber, tiles or carpet in the house?
- Should you go with white on white or colour?
- Is four smaller bedrooms better than three really big ones?

The key here is to really look at your market, and what product you are best suited to create, and then find the area where these two factors intersect.

You know how sometimes you walk into a home that is for sale and it feels a little bland, a little lifeless? This usually happens for the following two reasons:

- The person designing the interiors was too focused on what the market wants and, in an attempt to appeal to everyone, appeals to no-one as it becomes a little boring, too safe; it all blends and feels very vanilla, which has no draw or appeal.
- The person who makes the decisions on what should go where and how it will all come together is so afraid of making a decision that will turn people off that they again end up appealing to no-one.

So easy to do, right! I rarely actually see someone get it wrong because they have just chased their dream and decided the whole world wants a red kitchen with a lime green splashback. However, the conversation is so often around how you must not polarise — you must appeal to a mass market, you must dismiss your ideas because they might not be right for everyone.

I disagree.

A home should have personality and warmth. It should tell a story and while you want it to appeal to the majority of people, it will not be perfect for everyone. And that is good! You need to create an actual connection with a purchaser, one where they feel like this is their home, one that speaks to them. You want the conversation in the purchaser's head to be around how amazing the home you have built is and how they couldn't create one like this, or wouldn't have been brave enough to purchase stone like that, rather than them having a conversation in their head about what they could live with or how they would change the home over time.

This is liberating when you embrace it! It means that you can have a little, fun step into your happy place and play a game where you get to dictate the style and make decisions that you know will appeal to many (like the three vs four bedrooms debate) but also where you can shine a little and create a house that is a home — one that will be appreciated for the thought you have put behind each of the decisions you have made.

Case Study: Unlocking feasibilities

Project overview

Purchased	$815 000
Sold	$1 645 500
Time	10 months

Renovations and transformations are so much fun and this one is a cracker! Before stood a dark and dingy 1970s concrete block-work home, but after Taeler was finished, we have seen this transformed into an architecturally designed home which can adapt and change with a family over time. To do this, Taeler needed to 'unlock the floorplan'. Much of renovating for profit is the ability to see potential and Taeler could see potential in spades!

(continued)

Key changes to the property include

— Creating an entry out of a general-purpose room

— Opening up the entry to the street to create curb appeal

— Reconfiguring the home throughout to allow for a central hallway and plenty of light

— Adding a master suite so you feel like you are in a hotel

— Adding an extension that opened the existing home into a big family area with soaring ceilings and a cook's kitchen with a gorgeous outlook

— Creating a connection between the home and the backyard, with the addition of the cutest Plungie pool!

Taeler explains:

The home is primarily designed around the view of the landscape, architectural moments, and detail. The house is to be inviting warm and evoke feeling. Research is a beautiful leafy suburb. This property is very secluded on a quiet street.

The garden is the heart of the home, and that's the first thing you see when you enter. A beautiful internal courtyard holds a vertical garden providing a memory of what was once there. The external brickwork creeping its way in, the beautiful travertine paving bleeding its way in from the front porch to flooring. A space that provides privacy, security and a private garden. The terrarium is a beautiful small garden that provides an indoor-outdoor blurring of the lines. This created a space that was both practical for greeting guests, but gave privacy, with the added bonus of creating a beautiful architectural moment of delight. Walking through the timber portal you enter into the flexible or informal lounge.

The main axis of the house is from front to back, creating a visual spine to the house.

The window to the front frames the beautiful sculptural gumtree. While aligning with the double height glazed doors to the rear, which frame a large and beautiful tree. The track lighting is very intentional to create a visual line through the centre of the house. To also inform a gallery-like hallway space.

The challenges

Now, every renovation has its ups and downs, and building and renovating through COVID and beyond with trade and material shortages was no different!

— *Trades being reliable. It was a real struggle to find good trades in this climate.*

— *The existing brick veneer home was visually very solidly built. No cracks or signs of movement. The house built on a concrete stump was a solid foundation. When removing existing windows and making way for new ones, the brickwork began to move. It was so unstable (brick ties were not installed correctly) that we decided to remove all brickwork from the subfloor up. This resulted in a major design amendment 10 days into construction.*

— *Getting materials. It felt like whatever material we needed had a shortage at that time. Internal doors, aluminium, bricks, glass, plaster, the list goes on.*

When we met Taeler, she was finishing her home renovation and we clearly remember her setting her intentions — well, wouldn't you know it her one-year plan was achieved in only six short weeks, with a few bold and exciting moves and a pretty amazing pipeline of projects to come.

(continued)

Taeler's tips for making the most from your project:

Feasibility is King and always be open to change and sidestepping! Fear was the thing standing between backing myself. Once I found BuildHer [and the DevelopHer Program] they were the missing link to help me throughout the entire process. That alongside the community-based support!'

A quick recap

— A simple but key part of renovating for profit is spending less than you sell the property for. This means calculating all the costs before you begin.

— A feasibility study is a profit-and-loss statement for the project you are looking to build and the simplest way to ensure you will have a profit at the end of the project.

— To ensure your feasibility is accurate, make estimates based on the scope of works, materials and trades and use a checklist to ensure every key cost is allowed for.

— You have the power to manipulate the costs throughout the project. Don't stop evaluating your decisions and if there is a better, more effective and more cost-effective way to do things that will deliver the same or a superior product.

— Leveraging is the key to success and how you build wealth. Every dollar you have working for you to increase your property's value and your wealth is a cost for which you should see a return on investment (ROI).

— Choosing projects that align with your values and outcomes is important when it comes to looking at profitable projects.

Your vision: doing your due diligence

Before, during and while you head down the feasibility path you also need to be looking at your vision for each project. You'll want to check that this is something other people will want, and that the project will actually stack up.

Sometimes you might decide that you want to do something on a block of land or renovate in a certain way, when this isn't actually the best option.

So how do you know that your vision is right?

Sense checking your idea

I sense check my visions in the following ways:

1. Review local sales results.
2. Speak with local agents on the buyer pool and find out what they are asking for.

3. Look at sold properties and understand how hard or easy they were to sell. How many contenders were there?

4. Gauge market interest. What properties have the most traction?

5. Understand the area demographics and supply.

6. Consider reverse feasibility and suburb uplift.

1. Review local sales results

Look at the sale values for properties sold in the area you're looking at. What do they tell you about the idea you are proposing?

Now I want you to really think about this. Would you prefer to live in the sold house or the one in your vision? Why? What makes one better than the other? Why would you pay more for one over the other? Buying and selling houses is a really emotional time for people. It is a time of reassessment of their values and what they are looking for in a property, and it is a time where they are making big decisions about their future.

Why is this important? You need to appeal to what your purchaser wants and needs. You need to create a property that solves their problems and appeals to their values. Purchasers are easily spooked! It is hard to move house, it is hard to organise finance and it is hard to shop for a house.

Yes, sometimes you are in a rising market where purchasers seem to fight for any property, but then consider that you will also become a purchaser in this market so you will need to maximise your result and return to be able to buy into a market that is moving quickly.

Pro tip

Keep a spreadsheet with detailed notes on each property. This will help you spot patterns and make informed decisions. Consider including columns or use the comparable sales template.

Features to inspect include:

— *Location:* for example, proximity to schools, parks, shopping centres

— *Size:* for example, square footage, number of bedrooms and bathrooms

— *Condition:* for example, new, renovated, needs work

— *Unique features:* for example, swimming pool, large garden, open floor plan

— *Market performance:* time on the market and final sale price vs asking price.

By doing this, you can start to see what works and what doesn't in your specific market.

2. Speak with local agents

Local agents have a huge amount of knowledge. They are on the frontline showing and selling properties daily. They are also the ones who are going to need to show your home and sell it. But tread with caution as they are not the ones who are buying it and they can only rely on the information at hand.

Questions I like to ask agents who are selling houses in the area where I would like to purchase a house for renovation are:

— Which properties sold really well?

— Why did those ones have so much competition? What were people drawn to?

— What didn't they like?

- — What are people asking for that they can't find?
- — Is there a type of property that has lots of demand, or where buyers are fighting for this type of property?
- — What would you do?

While you are asking the agent all of these questions and getting their insight, remember that ultimately you need to be responsible for bringing your vision to life and using the information that they give you to create the best product that you possibly can, with the information you have at hand, within your budget.

It can be a bit tricky as you are in research phase and before you purchase you need to work out what your unrenovated project is valued at now. You also want to turn it into an ideal product in the future, which means being across two different product types in the one area. If you are speaking to an agent who has a lot of unrenovated house listings and may not be across the higher end sales for that suburb, you may need to seek out advice or thoughts from an agent who is well versed in this aspect of the market for their opinion. You will also need to be looking at and attending opens for both types of properties.

Pro tip

This is a really good time to gauge whether you would like to work with an agent or not! Do they have time for you? Will they invest a little in you without the guarantee of a reward? Selling houses is a long game of relationships. Agents need to build a rapport with clients over years, listening to what they want and need and helping them purchase. Some agents are of the opinion that a property will just sell itself; others will put the time and effort into making sure that it will sell.

Note: Once I have a set of plans I show them to the agent I intend to sell with and see what they think. They will give me feedback based on their experience, and based on this feedback I will either amend my plans and thoughts or stick with my path.

3. How easy or hard was a property to sell?

It also matters how easy or hard it was to sell a property. If I am renovating a property I would really like a situation where the property is easy to sell. Too many times I have seen properties sell for an amount that is a standout. One purchaser paid above the odds because they were really connected to it, or at the eleventh hour there was one sole buyer who negotiated, or it took weeks and weeks of negotiations to bring someone across the line.

When you are investing your time, energy and effort into a property, you want to set yourself up for a home run — a win that you can bank on (as much as possible).

Dig deeper into properties that have sold. Find out how long they were on the market and how many serious contenders there were before and after the sale. This analysis will give you a clearer picture of what buyers are willing to pay for and how quickly they are making decisions, and will serve as a sense check on the data that the agent has given you.

It's worth attending open houses and auctions. This firsthand experience is invaluable. Observe, take notes and ask intelligent questions without interfering with the agents' time with potential buyers.

There are a few things to note when analysing sold properties:

— *Buyer behaviour:* notice how buyers react to different features of the home.

— *Bidding wars:* pay attention to what sparks bidding wars and high engagement at auctions.

— *Questions asked:* What questions are buyers asking? These can indicate what is most important to them.

4. Gauge market interest

By this I mean attention, views, likes, enquiries!

Some properties are immediately striking. They get attention and there are lots of people at the opens. Why is this? Is it the photos? Is it the location? Is it the historic nature or street presence?

I asked some agents these exact questions with regard to two properties we own, in different areas.

One property that we were looking at as a comparable got a lot of inspections. The imagery was bold and striking, and the garden area was large. This particular property had been on the market earlier and had had a makeover done on it quickly. There was no interest and poor viewings earlier, and then, after the cosmetic reno plus new kitchen, there were a lot of viewings. The property was still compromised in that it was on a prominent corner and so of the many people who viewed it the buyer pool was still thin. But, it was interesting to dissect the images and see what people were drawn to.

The second property was glamourous, architectural and different in nature. It was a beautiful home that had a lot of media attention and also had a lot of inspection because of the stunning styling and striking architecture. This home struggled to sell well because the building inspections came up with some issues that spooked the high-end purchasers. The architectural style also meant that the layout was unusual and families with younger children struggled to connect with it and see value at that price point, when they could purchase a less architectural but bigger home for the same amount.

On face value, the sale results tell you nothing of the story behind the house — that is, what people liked and didn't like. This information is subjective and takes time to establish. It is time in the game — watching the market, what is working and what isn't — but also listening to the agents and the amazing information they provide.

Arrogance in property developers is not to be admired! The massive fails that I have watched have often come from people who think they know better than everyone else. They don't bother to do the research and they miss the detail on how people and families want and like to live. They are homes that lack soul and depth, and are quick fixes that feel not quite right and don't draw an emotional reaction from buyers.

Pro tip

You can create alerts for properties similar to your finished product. This way, you'll be notified of new listings and can track their performance in real time. Sometimes it is so easy to get focused on the fixer uppers that you can forget to track the finished compatibles, too, and by analysing these metrics, you can adjust your property's features or marketing strategy to align with what is currently trending.

You can see a lot of information on the online sites and even on social media listings. Metrics to monitor include:

— *number of views: high interest can indicate popular features or competitive pricing*

— *save and share rates: properties saved and shared frequently are likely hitting the mark with buyers.*

5. Understand area demographics and supply

Your property's success can depend heavily on the area's demographics and available amenities. Consider:

— *local schools:* are they well regarded and in demand? Properties in good school districts often fetch higher prices and sell faster

— *amenities:* how close are shops, public transport, parks and recreational facilities? Proximity to amenities can significantly enhance a property's appeal

— *growth trends:* is the suburb growing or declining? Look at historical data to understand the long-term prospects of the area

— *income trends:* what are the average incomes and how are they changing? Higher average incomes can indicate a more affluent buyer pool.

When researching, use local government and real estate websites to gather data on school ratings and catchment areas. Check transport websites for transport routes. Physically walk the streets and think about whether you would like to live in that location.

6. Consider reverse feasibility and suburb uplift

When you're trying to narrow down an area you really need to be looking at areas that have enough of a gap to work in. Unrenovated properties are selling at a low enough price that there is profit to be made compared to the sold properties.

A quick run-through of the unrenovated house price values on a comparable spreadsheet and then renovated or new house price values should help you determine whether there is a gap wide enough to cover the cost of purchasing and settling the property, renovating and holding costs, and sale costs. If I think there is enough of a gap in a market, I like to look for a few completed projects to do reverse feasibilities on.

What do I mean by reverse feasibility? I want to run the numbers backwards for a house that has been purchased and renovated to see if it looks like they made a profit. This means I am making a huge number of assumptions, but it is easy to do and gives me a great amount of insight.

Here are the steps:

1. *Find a property that has been newly renovated and sold recently.*

    I will use the example of a house in Brunswick. It sold for $2 500 000 on 22 June 2024.

2. *Find the purchase price and date.*

    Using *corelogic.com.au* I discovered that it was purchased for $1150 000 on 24 April 2022.

This gives me a gap to work out: I can see there was a purchase and significant uplift in a short period of time and I can also find the before and after images and floorplans to try to assess what work was completed.

In this case, I would guess that they knocked down the house and built a new house. The new house looks to be 288 m² based on the data I have and has three bedrooms, three bathrooms and a garage.

At this point I can run some basic numbers to guess what the build might have cost and what the other costs might have been. You can never know this information for sure, but you can make a guess to see if it would work or even how it would work.

Fill out a feasibility template with your best guesses to see if you think you would make a profit on this project based on your numbers. In this case, I have used $3000 per square metre for the rate of construction and just guessed all of the other costs — see figure 3.1 (overleaf).

Summary development costs		
Sale price (A)		
	Sale price (based on comparable case studies)	$2500000
Acquisition costs (B)	Site purchase price	$1150000
	All other acquisition costs	$65250
	Subtotal	**$1215250**
Development costs (C)	Design and permits	$46050
	Demolition costs	$20000
	Planning, services and authorities	$10000
	Construction	$864000
	Landscaping	$40000
	Contingency	$0
	Contribution fees	$0
	Subtotal	**$980050**
Holding and sell costs (D)	Holding costs	$90000
	Sell costs	$49500
	Subtotal	**$139500**
Net profit		**$165200**

Figure 3.1: Estimated development costs for the Brunswick property

Here's a link to an online calculator on my website: www .buildhercollective.com.au/bookfreebies

Looking at these numbers, it seems they might have made a profit of $165200 on this project in this time frame. Again, I have no idea of the actual numbers — I am merely guessing to see if it looks like there has been value created. I can also play around with the costs and see what difference this makes in reverse, without pressure, as it is just research. What if we reduced the construction cost, or increased it? What if we used a more expensive or less expensive design team?

Justifying your value proposition

So often we get wrapped up in our own heads, creating a product that we think is right because it suits our situation. When we started out, my partner John and I renovated a house. We were living in it with five young children. We thought we might have a product that split families would like or be interested in as we had six bedrooms. We had purchased it as our home and renovated it bit by bit, and had overlooked the fact that it was on a main road, and near an intersection with a bus stop out the front. We knew it was easy to park and there wasn't a lot of noise because we lived there. Basically, we loved our home and had rose-coloured glasses on when we were looking at it.

Sometimes you need to remove yourself from the intimate relationship we tend to have with our ideas and justify your thoughts by putting them on paper and doing a little bit of critical analysis. This means you take each of the above steps and try to fairly and impartially work through them as an exercise on paper and then for bonus points explain or justify your thoughts to someone who knows.

At the point when you are justifying your value proposition, you have decided on a floorplan and have a clear idea of what direction you're heading in. The next steps are:

1. Complete the comparable properties sheet with notes.

2. Relook at your sales value from the viewpoint of a purchaser and what inclusions and features might draw them in.

3. Meet with an agent or someone who knows the area to sense check your thoughts on the value you are creating based on the sales. I find this step is best done when you have a floorplan and a few mood board pictures to explain your vision.

For all of my projects, when I have a clear direction on my floorplan I meet with the agent I'm working with to sell the property (yes, I decide this early) and talk through what I'm looking to take to market and whether this, in their opinion, covers everything that it needs to. A good agent will be able to read the plan well and give you guidance on things you may be able to improve on.

For one of my projects, I showed the agent my plans for the knock-down rebuild and he thought the master suite should be at the back of the house, not the front, that I needed additional storage and that the pool house was needed (I was weighing up which way I should go with this). So I adjusted my plans to incorporate the feedback and to meet market needs. Having met with him early in the design process meant there was still an opportunity to make adjustments.

For another project, the agent thought the main bathroom could be bigger (I agreed but couldn't change it due to the size of the house) and that the mudroom, kitchen and laundry set-up was ideal. While this didn't result in any changes, it did give me an understanding that I was on the right path.

Choosing your moment

This is not the fun chapter where I show you how to pick the market. I won't be getting out my crystal ball and waving my magic wand to head off into the future and back again to tell you how we guarantee we are buying at the bottom of the market and that we can sell at the top of the market.

No, this is the chapter where I talk about the numbers in the market we are in and how to move forward with these. You can only play in the market you are currently in. Over the years, too many people have talked to me about what they will be doing and about factoring in some growth in the market to make their numbers stack up, but this is not how I play the game.

Why? Well, you can't work into the future because you don't know what will happen. Will there be an event that changes the game and makes everything trade higher — like the lockdowns did in the Melbourne higher end housing market — or lower, like the GFC did? With this in mind you will need to run your numbers as at now and increase the value of your home now.

If you do a renovation and it is predicted to add $200 000 to the bottom line now, then the value will have increased no matter if the entire market rises or falls. If you are in this game for the long term and the market rises by $100 000, then yippee! This means you will have made $300 000.

However, the next time you go to buy, your buy-in price will also be $100 000 more, so this money is not really realised. It is the same for a falling market. If the market contracts by $100 000 and you are selling for a $100 000 profit, then in theory the next property you buy will also be $100 000 cheaper … and the show goes on.

When talking to builders about how many out of 10 projects go well, they would expect around one in ten to knock it out of the park, to fly and yield a completely unexpected high profit. You know, those ones where people are fighting it out at the auction to buy the property and it sells for way more than you thought. Seven of them will do pretty much what they are meant to do and two of them may feel harder than the others. The game is a game you play over time. It is important to note that this probably won't make you $1 million in a year without having a bit of equity behind you (although I have seen it happen).

Let's look at the difference between playing now and waiting.

Saving 10 per cent

Let's say you work and save 10 per cent of your money for 10 years. Assuming an average salary is $98 000, and the approximate after-tax amount is $75 852. If you save 10 per cent of your take-home pay, you will be saving $7585 per year for 10 years. Adding in a compounding factor of 10 per cent, you can expect to have saved $121 145 at the end of this period, as detailed in figure 3.2 (overleaf).

(continued)

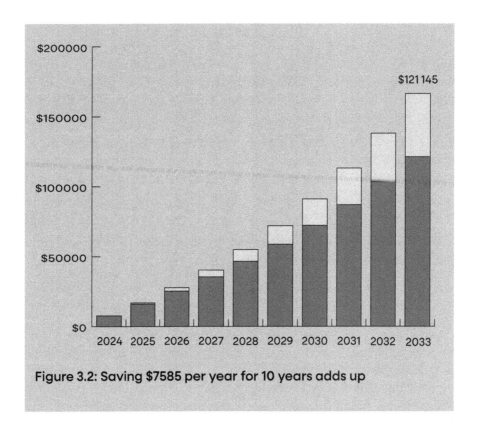

Figure 3.2: Saving $7585 per year for 10 years adds up

Now let's say you were able to make a return of $200 000 over two years because you did one renovation every two years on top of your job. (Please understand I have seen people consistently make more than this amount in many markets). Let's also assume this is not your primary residence and you intend to renovate for profit, so you would be paying capital gains tax (CGT) on your profit. Working through the CGT calculator on the ATO website, here's what you would be looking at.

The results of renovating

If your capital proceeds are $200 000 per project and you apply for a CGT discount of 50 per cent as you have held the property for more than 12 months (and assuming you are eligible: please check on the ATO website).

On the assumption you are taxed at the top marginal income tax rate, these would be the results:

Project return	$200 000
Capital gain on the property in 24 months	$200 000
CGT discount (capital gain x 50 per cent)	$100 000
CGT discounted rate x 45 per cent	$45 000 tax payable
Profit after tax (capital gain — tax payable)	$155 000

If you did this five times in the ten years — each time saving and banking your profits earning the same 10 per cent return on your investment that we used in the savings example — you would be looking at having created $775 000 from doing these renovations and the total value over time with the 10 per cent rate would be $1 293 967 (see figure 3.3).

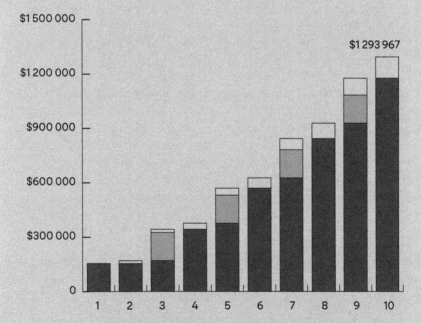

Figure 3.3: Saving your profits five times in 10 years adds up

So, will your numbers roll out exactly like this?

No! I can almost guarantee it. However, the point is that by actively working your money, and growing your funds by renovating for profit, you can create the kind of wealth that you can't create just by saving. The time and effort you invest in doing the work of renovating projects is giving you the outweighed financial return you will receive.

This return should be there regardless of the rise and fall of the market, as the market will keep moving, ebbing and flowing, regardless of what actions you will take. The important thing here is that you continue playing the game over time.

I have watched would-be renovators and investors wait more than 10 years for the 'right' time to buy while they deliberate, and lament that everything is too expensive and overpriced. Dwelling values rose by 67.5 per cent over the 10 years to December 2023, according to *corelogic.com.au*, and inflation rose by 29.1 per cent over the same period, seeing an average increase in house prices of 56.8 per cent. These numbers show that it is not easier to get into the market by waiting it out.

To give these numbers context: a property worth $500 000 in 2013 would be worth $740 740 in 2023, on average, and I am sure that we can all think of places where the market far exceeded this growth. Still, even with a 56.8 per cent increase in value, over 10 years of passive investment this property is unlikely to help you retire. However, by jumping in and creating value you are able to vastly increase your wealth over this period of time.

While we cannot pick the market — and, in my opinion, no-one will ever be able to pick the market perfectly — we can read the market movements a bit, understanding some of the indicators that are at play to read what is happening in different market segments.

Here's what I look for:

- *Lower-than-average sales volumes* — a sluggish market where clearance is not happening at all of the auctions.
- *Price reductions on properties* — sometimes it is worth looking at the properties that have sat on the market for

the longest time. Often they need a real price reduction to get things moving and — depending on why it has passed in or not moved — could mean good opportunities.

— *Properties sitting on the market for a long time* — this is when that 'average days on market' pushes out.

— *Low consumer sentiment* — this is an interesting one because it is something you can feel before you can see. It is when the power shifts to the purchasers and there is a lack of fear of missing out (FOMO). The economists have a number of data-driven stats they are looking at for sentiment. The thing to understand is the shift in feeling – who has the power, vendor or purchaser?

— *Fear in the market* — when the media is selling fear and purchasers lack optimism, it can be a good time to buy.

— *The balance of power being with purchasers* — when you are buying, this is really great, but not so much when you are selling. However, great properties will always move.

But there are issues with this. Sentiment is low, so no-one wants to buy. And as much as you know not to do what everyone else is doing, buying when people are not buying is hard to get your head around. Basically, this is the fear that is stopping everyone from moving forward. The forces that exist on the market can also put pressure on you and it can be hard to not feel this fear.

My advice is to play the game consistently and not try to pick the market highs and lows. If you're looking at an area, what do you need to look for as a base? What are some of the markets of an area where renovating for profit will work — and beware because it doesn't work everywhere in every market!

Simply put: look for the gap.

The gap between unrenovated and renovated houses is the best indicator to me that there could be money to be made. If unrenovated houses are selling at close to the value of renovated houses, it may be very hard to play the game in that market with all the other on-costs to consider, such as stamp duty, and holding and selling costs.

So, we are looking for a gap between the newly built or renovated homes and the unrenovated. With a broad brushstroke back-of-envelope calculation, there needs to be money left on the table for profit. Remember, we are starting with a very simple calculation in the initial phases. If it doesn't work as a simple calculation, it definitely won't work when you add on all the costs.

These are often areas where they have smaller land so the building costs are lower overall as the builds aren't as big but where the land value is higher, so the value of your house build proportional to the land is smaller. An example of this is the cost of building on a 400 m^2 piece of land in the inner city is similar to in the outer suburbs, but on the 400 m^2 home you may only need to add 100 m^2 of building to have a big home. However, in the outer suburbs where homes are bigger, the expectation might be to build an additional 200 m^2, which would put the cost of building up proportional to the land. The difference is the cap on the end sale price in that area and what people are willing to pay for.

What if you can't afford to buy in an area that will be profitable? Well, this will come down to how you finance the build, which can also be fun and creative. Most of us don't start with a pile of money. We need to earn it, so we need to build up our profits as we continue along the journey of renovating for profit. Smaller projects often take less time, but can be less profitable, so you may need to do a few of them to get started. Or you may need to sell the home you are living in and move to a new one in the initial phases as you are building up your equity and leveraging the savings you have available. This is the bit where people bow out: they don't want to make a sacrifice, so they never take the first steps.

A quick recap

Be clear on your vision and crosscheck your assumptions in the following ways.

— Check the sold values of comparable properties, physically listing some of their inclusions and exclusions.

— Check with agents on how deep the buyer pool is. Is there scarcity around availability. What are they looking for that is not being hit by the market? What could you do to create the perfect property?

— Critically re-assess the comparable sold properties and understand how hard or easy they were to sell. How many contenders were there, both before they were renovated and after? You may need to chase down agents and start a relationship with them to get this information. Turning up at auctions and opens yourself and combining this with knowledge taken from trusted agents will help you put together a great snapshot of the situation.

— What is driving interest from the market? What properties have the most traction? Which ones have people turning up? What was it about marketing and presentation that created this drive? Understand what is the secret sauce of the properties that sell exceedingly well.

— Who is in this area? What is the average income? What do the families look like? Is the ratio of families to family homes being built in check?

— You can use reverse feasibilities to ratify numbers and check you are on the right path.

Financing and funding: the basics

Parts of this chapter were created and written in collaboration with and by our partners in mortgage broking, Entourage. You can reach out to them and get access to some great calculators and tools here: www.entourage.com.au/buildher

Managing cash flow and funds is the key to a smooth build. There are many ways to increase your funds within the property cycle, but when you are caught short without warning it can become really stressful. This means you will want to balance the amount of cash you have available and how you are funding the purchase and the renovation to give yourself maximum flexibility.

Funding the purchase of your build

Finance and the lending environment can change really quickly. The banks' appetite for lending, rates and requirements is always in a mild state of flux, so I have found the best way to navigate the process and understand the current environment is to work with a broker who can secure funding and workshop scenarios. If you are looking to build and renovate for profit, you will usually look to secure funding so it is important that you understand the way this works from the banks' perspective. You'll want to understand how you can operate within the different products they have available.

Working out how much of your own money you will need and how much you can borrow will be one of the keys to determining what type of property you can purchase. We will run through the details shortly, but basically, you will need to fund the following:

— deposit

— remainder of the property value to settle

— costs to settle

— cost of interest as you build

— cost of the renovation works

— cost of marketing and styling.

For example, if I was able to get a loan at 80 per cent for a property that I purchased for $850 000 and I was doing a renovation over 12 months that will cost $250 000, then my situation might look like this.

Loan ($850 000 x 80 per cent)	**$680 000**
Interest, based on 6.3 per cent, P&I ($4205 × 12)	**$50 460**
Deposit ($850 000 x 20 per cent)	$170 000
Settlement costs (stamp duty, mortgage registration fee, transfer fee, conveyancing) in Victoria	+ $51 000
Renovation works	+ $250 000
Cost of marketing and styling	+ $13 000
Total cash required	$484 000

The cash I would require if I was borrowing 80 per cent of the cost of the property would be all of the above except for the loan and interest costs, so would be equal to $484 000, and then I would need to allow for running costs such as water, electricity and council rates.

If I was able to borrow the cost of the renovation using construction finance I may only need $234 000. But I would have additional interest repayments associated with the increased borrowings.

An understanding of how to structure your loans to work around the cash you have available is really important to be able to leverage this aspect of the build.

I will look to break down some of the components of finance and funding in this chapter. However, you will need to get personal advice from a broker that relates specifically to your situation.

The deposit

Whether you've bought before or not, when buying property you'll be required to contribute to the purchase costs by way of a deposit. You can choose to fund this deposit in a couple of different ways depending on your financial structure.

The minimum amount of deposit you usually need to purchase a property is 20 per cent plus costs. You can borrow more than 80 per cent of the purchase price in some circumstances but often the bank will then require that you pay lenders mortgage insurance (LMI), which can be very expensive. LMI is the premium paid to the lender's mortgage insurer and it protects the lender you have borrowed from, not you, in the event that you default on your loan.

If a great opportunity arises and you don't have a 20 per cent deposit, then LMI can provide you with the means to acquire the property with a lesser deposit. This is common for first home buyers — it gets them into the market and gives them the opportunity to start building their asset base with a lower barrier to entry.

If you have cash savings, you may choose to contribute this to your property purchase. Alternatively, if you have an existing property that has increased in value or that you have equity in, then you might choose an equity release. This is where you release the equity within a property by redrawing funds, or increase an existing loan facility to contribute towards your next purchase.

Once you've got your deposit sorted, the next question is how much the bank will lend you.

Pro tip

These days it is very common to offer a 10 per cent deposit in the terms. This can even be negotiated prior to an auction as part of your terms if you do secure the property.

How is borrowing power calculated?

Your borrowing power determines how much the bank is comfortable lending you. It is based on your current financial situation and the interest rates at the time of borrowing. These fluctuate and change based on the economic environment.

So how do the banks calculate what they will lend? They look at your income and your cost of living and calculate what you have available to repay a mortgage. The banks must make reasonable inquiries about a customer's requirements, objectives and financial situation under the *National Credit Act*. They do this in a number of ways, but here is a list of factors that impact borrowing power:

— income

— living expenses

— dependants

— existing loans

— other debt (like HECS)

— credit card limits (not just the outstanding balance)

— overall debt-to-income ratio

— current interest rate

— making principal and interest repayments versus interest only

— assessment rate.

It is important to note that different lenders will apply different weightings to the above factors, which will mean that each lender will offer a different loan amount based on its internal assessment process and risk appetite. This is why I like to use a broker as they have access to each of the individual lender's calculators. Early on in my journey I sought to borrow by approaching the banks directly and was told I could not borrow the amount I needed by at least three different lenders. But with me being my best determined self, I met a broker who was able to take me through the process and match my situation with a lender that would work with me. This was an absolute game changer and completely unlocked my life from that point forward.

So how can you improve your borrowing power if you are meeting this as a blocker? In any situation, neither a broker nor a bank is going to encourage you to put yourself in a position where you are stretched to your limit. A loan needs to be suited to you and your lifestyle. This is why serviceability exists: to ensure you are not borrowing more than you can repay.

That said, there are ways you can improve your maximum borrowing power within the limits of the lending architecture.

Reduce your existing debt

This is the best way to go about increasing your borrowing power. For example, reducing a credit card limit by $20 000 can increase your borrowing capacity for a property by almost $100 000. Even if your credit card is not used and has been stuck in the bottom draw for emergencies only, lenders will take into their calculations the entire limit as if it were debt owing at the credit card interest rates. Lenders look at the limit you have so they can see what your maximum exposure would be. At one stage I had a credit card with a limit of $55 000 that needed to be reduced to $12 500 to allow for my borrowing capacity to work. Now, to be clear, I did not have that card maxed out, but when building and renovating it can be handy to have a card with a lot of money available. For example, when you are ordering concrete they keep a card on file and charge you each time a load leaves the depot — and if you're buying $30 000 of concrete it can add up to a lot of transferring!

Reduce your living expenses

Things like negotiating your insurance premiums, utilising rewards points and programs, and swapping energy providers can help. If the bank is reviewing your statements it would be wise to reduce your discretionary spending too, which will include all those non-essentials like eating out, shopping and holidays in the lead-up to applying for the loan.

Increase your income

Of course, if it were as easy as that, we'd all do it! For some people who are self-employed it might mean reducing deductions to boost earnings. For those who are employees, asking for a pay rise or starting a side-hustle might be a way. If you do decide to moonlight as an Uber driver, most lenders will want you to demonstrate 1 to 2 years' proof of income before the bank will use it. Work with your broker on what you need to increase your income and how you might demonstrate this.

Buy with a partner

If you're buying an investment property, buying with another trusted person may be a good solution. This could be a family member, business partner or friend. Seeking legal advice prior to commencing will be important, as this protects your and their interests and sets out the terms of the relationship from the beginning. Before you go down this path it is important to understand their situation and their capacity to service the debt. If you are planning on borrowing again before you have sold the property you will also need to understand the structure as some of the banks will look at the entire debt as yours to repay and if it is rented, only half of the income.

• • •

Once you know how much the lender is prepared to offer, the next step would be to get a pre-approval in place to allow you to negotiate or bid confidently. You can bid and secure a property without a pre-approval, but if you don't have a finance clause in place and you can't get funding then you could land yourself in hot water.

Credit files

The lender you are working with will access your credit file when they are assessing you. It is worth having a look at your file before you apply to borrow money. The way the credit file works in Australia is different from other countries — the way the data is collected and reported continues to evolve over time and has recently become a lot more current and integrated. At the time of writing there is a small number of private firms (not legislated by the government) that will hold this information, and the way it is assessed is different for each organisation.

Your credit file will contain information on you such as your name, date of birth, address and employer. It also includes information on your financial history. Your mortgages, credit cards and even phone bills will be listed. These days banks even report on whether you are paying your debts on time or late — and, if the latter, by how many days. They may also have information about when you have failed to meet obligations or have had defaults.

Every time you apply for credit and that provider accesses your credit report it will be listed as an enquiry along with the value of that enquiry (even if you don't go ahead with getting the credit). Too many credit requests will be a red flag and may eventually cause an issue with getting credit. If you apply for loans and they are not approved, this will be recorded; if you are using afterpays that access your credit report, they will be recorded as well. The same goes for other providers, such as utility providers. It is important that you do not let too many people access this report as too many credit applications or requests that have been denied will make it harder to be approved for credit.

What does this mean for you? Pay your bills on time — automated payments are the best! Make sure you understand what is on your file so if there are any issues they can be cleared up before you get into a stressful situation with a bank.

I had a loan application that didn't proceed in the final hour. Following this, there was another application that wasn't a match due to something undisclosed by another party on the loan. When I then completed a third finance application, the lenders were concerned and queried why the other loans didn't proceed. You can see from this example how it is important to keep your record as clear as possible.

Pre-approval

Auctions are final and if you are the successful bidder, you need to pay your deposit on the spot. If you haven't negotiated subject to finance or secured a pre-approval, then you may be leaving yourself exposed. During private negotiations, even without a pre-approval, if the vendor accepts, you may be able to make the offer subject to finance approval, which ensures a level of protection in the event the lender isn't prepared to approve the loan (or if they offer a lesser amount than is required to complete the sale). These finance clauses are normally for a set period of time, like 10 working days. However, even if it is your strategy to put a clause in that is 'subject to finance' the vendor may not be willing to accept this clause and if you are in a market where there are two similar offers, the one that is subject to finance will be less favourable. Personally, when selling a home I am wary of subject to finance clauses and would only take one if I had no alternative or it was an amazing deal.

A pre-approval will provide you with peace of mind that the lender has looked at your actual financial situation (not just a rough one input in a serviceability calculator), and completed a credit assessment, which includes a credit check and a peek at your expenses too. If you don't have time to do this, or you haven't managed to work through the process and the perfect house comes up, then you have a decision to make around your capacity for risk and ability to solve the problem.

There are two types of pre-approval. A desktop pre-approval is based on the information input into an online calculator — which will often include a credit check, but is not actually assessed by a person — and a fully assessed pre-approval, which is just that: a thorough look at your situation including payslips, bank statements, debt and credit statements, credit check and identification. If you receive a fully assessed pre-approval you can negotiate and bid with confidence, knowing the lender has looked at everything and approved you subject to the property being acceptable.

Interest rates

I understand that interest rates worry people and while I aim to keep the interest repayments as low as possible, I am also realistic in that it is a cost of working in this industry. Often when interest rates are sitting higher, the property values are sitting lower, which gives me a greater uplift when I sell. The aim is to move property quickly and not hold onto it for too long. If you are unable to borrow the amount required to fund the renovation on a lower interest rate, then I would be looking to a different product.

I mentioned above that each lender has different criteria for how they assess your situation — sometimes, for example, there are products that are a better fit, like a low-doc product for someone who is self-employed.

Offset accounts

One of my favourite products to have alongside my home loans, offset accounts enable me to have cash sitting against the total loan amount so I am only paying interest on the remaining amount. Having funds sitting in an offset account means that I have the freedom to withdraw them whenever I see fit, but I also have the benefit of that money reducing the value of the mortgage.

When borrowing, I will generally seek to maximise my borrowings, tipping in as little cash as possible, and place the remaining funds that I will require to renovate or improve the property in an offset account. This also means it is more efficient to build as I have more options with how I structure the contracts and I don't need to pay for consultants to review contracts and verify work along the way.

Here's an example of how this might work.

How offset accounts work

For a property that costs $850 000, I have $500 000 available to complete the project. Instead of contributing all of the money I have and then asking to borrow it again to do the construction, I would borrow the maximum possible, which is $680 000, and put the remainder of the funds required to renovate and build in the offset account. This amount is approximately $313 000 ($250 000 for the build, $13 000 for the styling and marketing, and $50 000 for the interest). This reduces my loan to $367 000 and the interest payable will be calculated on this amount. I can draw funds as I require them to build and have the benefit of the cash in the interim.

Of course, this would require having cash to fund the deposit, settlement, interest, construction, styling and marketing. If this is not the case, then I might require construction finance.

Equity release

Equity release means accessing the equity that you have in a property. Equity is essentially the difference between the value of the property and what you owe on the loan. For example, if you own a property worth $1 000 000 and owe $400 000 on your mortgage, then you have $600 000 in equity. As we have seen, lenders will not let you access the full amount of equity. However, you can usually access up to 80 per cent provided you can service the loan.

So, to work through the above example.

Property value	**$1 000 000**
Mortgage amount	$400 000
Equity remaining	$600 000
Amount of equity available (property value × 80 per cent minus existing loan)	**$400 000**

When you are arranging an equity release on your loan, lenders will ask you what you are planning to use the funds for. There may be a limit the lender will allow you to borrow to put towards your renovation without having to provide additional evidence such as a copy of your building contract or other documentation. They may even ask you to revert to a construction loan.

This is one of the reasons I prefer to maximise out borrowing in the initial phase and use an offset account to hold the funds until I am ready to use them. Having control of the cash to manage the build is very helpful.

Construction and renovation finance

A construction loan is specifically designed to be paid out at predetermined steps or stages throughout the building process. The stages are generally in accordance with a construction contract. This type of loan is usually set to interest only while the build or renovation is taking place, then reverts to principal and interest upon completion.

It's a good idea to work with a broker to navigate the process of obtaining a construction loan and how much you can borrow. Your mortgage broker will let you know exactly what's required, but it usually involves providing a signed fixed-price build contract, plans and specifications, and any quotes for additional items being financed as part of the construction (such as landscaping and pools).

It is important to note that while there are exceptions, most banks will only lend where you have a construction contract in place and a quantity surveyor, who is an independent consultant working for the bank, has verified these figures. The bank will also expect you to get an 'as if' complete valuation to determine an estimate of what the final value will be once your construction is completed and to ensure your property continues to have the required equity.

Once approved, you'll be able to pay your deposit to the builder (usually 5 per cent of your building contract price). The lender will pay in accordance with the stages of the building contract. This will differ for each builder and bank, but will generally follow this format.

Deposit	5 per cent
Slab	15 per cent
Frame	20 per cent
Lock-up	20 per cent
Fit-out	30 per cent
Completion	10 per cent

You will need to provide documentation at each stage. This might be an invoice and a statutory declaration from the builder. You may require a site inspection too.

There are a few things to note:

— Most lenders will expect you to work with a registered builder. The implication here is that you will struggle to obtain a construction loan if you are an owner-builder, even if you are a registered builder yourself.

— You will normally need to have a fixed-price contract in place with your builder. Banks assess risk, and this type of contract de-risks the project because a fixed-price contract means the builder agrees to cover any costs that arise above the price agreed upon in the contract. If you make any variations to the build outside of the contract, then you'll be liable to cover them, which may mean having to go back to the bank to ask for more funds.

Substituting equity

When you buy and sell properties regularly, with some products you can sometimes substitute the equity. This means that you are able to move your loan from one property to another property without going through the entire application process again.

Let's say you sold the property that you purchased for $850 000 and decided to buy another one around the same time. You sell the property for $1 550 000 and make a profit of $320 000 after all is said and done. It has been a good project and you want to do it again, having found another property that you can purchase for $950 000. Your existing loan of $680 000 is less than 20 per cent so you should be able to move the loan across without completing servicing.

There are some important acts to understand about substituting equity:

— Not all banks allow it.

— Some banks will allow you to hold funds for a period of time; others require settlements to align to be able to move the loan. Lining up settlements can be a challenge to orchestrate.

— Lenders will generally ask that you are not increasing the total dollar value of the loan and that the LVR (loan-to-value ratio) remains on or under what it was previously. The LVR was originally 20 per cent in this case, so they would not allow that to drop to 10 per cent if you purchased something cheaper.

Development finance

Some projects might be suitable for development finance. This is where you do not need to show serviceability; rather, you need to establish that the project is profitable. These loans are generally used for subdivision projects, but I have also used them to fund new builds or projects where there are multiple investors and servicing would be very challenging.

Development finance is a particular type of finance and there are various lenders available to service this market. It generally costs more than standard finance and has a different set of requirements. The lender will assess you as an individual — your track record and what you have achieved to date — and also the project — its costs, timelines, proposal, feasibility study and ROI.

There will be more documentation required and an upfront line fee, which can be 1 to 2 per cent before interest hits. The LVR would typically sit lower, around 60–70 per cent, and if there is a multi-lot subdivision in question, then you may need to show presales. It generally funds like a construction project with the difference being that you can sometimes capitalise interest, so you won't pay interest monthly for a period of time while you are developing. This interest, however, will be applied and drawn down in total before your build costs are funded

I wanted to mention that while development finance is a source of funding that is available, I haven't gone into too much detail as it will not fit most projects that are renovations and it is a more expensive way to fund a project; however, for the right project it is a game changer as you will not need to demonstrate serviceability on feasible projects, which can be a limitation as your project size and borrowings grow.

Private investors

Consider private investors as an alternative. There are private investing companies and individuals that might consider lending you money towards your project. An individual private lender could be a friend, family member or business that is known to you, or it could be a company that specialises in these types of projects.

Private lenders may be easier to work with than a big bank, but then they also might have a different set of strings attached. I have known women who have successfully used private lending as a source of funds for the renovation portion of their project. This has allowed them to access traditional finance for one portion of the project and to keep playing the game where they might not have otherwise been able to play. This type of funding can be particularly helpful if you have unexpected and unanticipated costs.

Case Study: Renovating over time and releasing equity

Project overview

Purchase Price	$880 000
Price Sold	$2 085 000
Cost of Works Completed	$520 000
Date of Project	2020–2023
Type of Project	Renovation and double storey extension

Elise completed the restoration of a Victorian façade home, and renovation of the first three rooms of the home, before they refinanced to release equity to complete an extension on the rear of the home.

This strategy is very helpful in growing equity as, provided your renovation increased the value of the home, you can redraw this money again to complete more work. You will want to speak to your broker about how you structure this as it relies on capacity to service the loan and a bank valuation.

After the initial renovation of the façade and first three rooms, Elise and her partner Sam then completed the demolition of a 70s lean to the extension completed by the previous owners. They then built a double storey extension consisting of an open plan kitchen, living, dining, laundry, butlers, master, WIR and ensuite, retreat, study, balcony and alfresco. They were also able to fit out as a studio an old workshop at the rear of the property. This studio included a kitchen, bathroom and bedroom which they lived in while they were working on their home.

Elise's thoughts going into the project

We were really excited to do a renovation. We had previously completed a new build and were ready for a

(continued)

different challenge. We were probably naïve (in a good way?) to how large the project we were planning would become as we were completing it as owner-builders. It was actually a blessing that we didn't realise how big of a project it was for us as we may not have had such a good result if we had reduced our plans.

Things that went really well

We renovated in two stages. Renovate the existing part of the home that we would keep, then complete the extension. This was a less efficient way of completing the project but it was the key to obtaining the funds for the extension. When we had the house revalued after stage one was complete, our financing for the extension was locked in. That was a massive milestone.

As we both are in the building industry we managed the project effectively. This meant that once we had the funds for the extension the project really flew. We had it all planned and procured to ensure everything and everyone that was required on-site was there when we needed. There was no downtime waiting because someone had forgotten to order something or didn't book in the plumber. We were able to complete the double storey extension in 7 months whereas the renovation of the front of the house took 2 years as we were doing things on top of work, and as we saved money.

What didn't go so well

Our sewer pipe in the driveway got filled with gravel right at the end of the project and had to be replaced. It was fixable but a large cost we did not need so late in the project. Thank goodness for contingency!

Learnings from project

Planning is key. Make your decisions early, check lead times for all of the building materials and trades.

It is a lot more efficient to build if you can do everything all at once. Living in the renovation and moving room to room created a lot of extra work and took a lot longer.

Don't sweat the small stuff. There were lots of little details we spent a lot of time deliberating on. In the end, no-one noticed them and so much time and effort went into them. A project is better done than perfect!

What's next

We have purchased our next project which is another single front weatherboard house. We are currently in the design concept phase with plans to commence construction in January 2025.

Using collaboration to build profitable joint ventures

One of the ways people start out, or continue, to build, renovate and develop with more projects in what can be a competitive market is by using joint ventures (JVs), which effectively means two or more people or parties come together to work on a project. I like JVs, particularly because they offer a powerful avenue for combining resources, expertise and networks to achieve outcomes that would not be possible alone.

A JV is a strategic partnership formed between two or more parties with the objective of pursuing a specific business endeavour, or in our case, a building project. In the context of building projects, JVs enable you to pool resources, knowledge and capabilities to tackle ventures that may be beyond the scope of individual entities. JVs can take various forms, such as contractual agreements, limited partnerships or equity JVs, depending on the desired level of collaboration and shared risk.

Most often, when people are starting out in JVs, they will be between two known parties, such as family members (my first joint venture was with my sister). These parties will come together to build or renovate, splitting and sharing the costs and the profits between them.

JVs have been very popular in our DevelopHer group lately and, honestly, I can see why: there are many benefits. This is a method of raising funds and building projects that I have seen many property developers and groups of men use over the years, but I have rarely seen women come together to complete projects like this.

I love them in the right situation! I know and have seen the benefits that they can bring to projects and wealth creation. I have also seen some scenarios where there have been issues or changes of circumstances that have been less than ideal.

In some ways, JVs are more risky than doing projects by yourself. In other ways, however, you can use JVs to diversify and share your risk.

Types of JVs

There are many different project types and structures that you can undertake and each one will use a different set-up. So, it is important to get some legal advice around how to structure JVs. The scale of the project, timelines and contributions will dictate the most appropriate structure style. It is important to remember that there are many ways these can be set up and so many different types of contributions that can be made. Here are some of the ways we have seen them work really well in our community.

Renovating-for-profit JVs between close parties

This might be appropriate if you and a family member come together to pool your funds, purchase a home, renovate it and sell it again. You will ideally have a contract that details both parties' roles and responsibilities and outlines how to mitigate risk or work through any unknowns. In this scenario, both parties might contribute the same or different resources to the project and you may use a contractual partnership or an equity JV to complete this project.

Investment into an arm's length JV

Consider the scenario where you invest capital into a project that is being set up, run and completed by a third party. This may be where a party has a project running and one or a number of investors to contribute funds, with a proposal on how much return they should expect to see on their money. It is important that you understand the project, its risks and a number of potential outcomes before you invest in this type of scenario.

Seller JVs

You might think about a seller JV as one idea here — for example, one party has a property that they would like to sell that would benefit from a renovation; another has knowledge and expertise on how to drive the profits on this project. The two parties will enter into a contract that outlines the terms and contributions, including but not limited to the agreed value of the home, cash required to renovate, selling scenarios, timelines and all the nitty gritty of the details.

Why people like JVs

The main drivers I have found are:

- They can be fun!
- You can share the cost of a project (lower costs up front).
- You can get started straight away (if you don't have enough money to do so on your own).
- You can diversify your investments, rather than throwing all your funds into one deal.
- Bigger projects can be possible — beyond what your budget will allow.
- You'll learn from your JV partners, have an opportunity to collaborate and gain access to new knowledge, skills and expertise.

- You can combine resources and divide up the tasks based on experience. Also, more people means more hands on deck to deliver the work.
- You can share the risks and liabilities.
- You can set up your own structure to maximise your tax / profit opportunities.
- It's a temporary arrangement.
- It can help grow your business by being involved in more projects at the same time.

Setting up a JV

The chicken or the egg — is it the property first, or establishing a group first?

We have gotten to know each other a little over the course of this book, so you probably already know I don't want to, or couldn't, answer this one with a blanket response. Setting up a JV and how you do it really depends on what you are doing, where and with whom. There are pros and cons to each of the options, which I address in tables 4.1 and 4.2. Ultimately, you will need to get clarity on what you want from the group and who they might be before you determine the outcome. If you are looking to do a JV with a family member, the process might be a little easier and quicker.

Table 4.1: The pros and cons of doing a property-first JV

Pros	Cons
Having an understanding of the project, feasibility and dollars required	Time pressure to find a JV group
Working out projected roles, location and time frames	If you need to purchase in your name and then find the group, the onus is on you as the purchaser

Table 4.2: The pros and cons of doing a group-first JV

Pros	Cons
You have time to work through how it might work, the dollars available and how to put the group together	Searching can be arduous as a group and it can take a while to find a project that stacks up
You can look, as a group, at properties that might work for all of you and learn about how you all work together	The project that works might not fit your ideals and might change the structure at the last minute
When you purchase, you purchase in a group with a known entity	

Sometimes 'pros and cons' lists are helpful, but sometimes they really just offer a list without application.

Here is an overview of how I found some of my JV projects and how they have come together.

Example joint ventures (JVs)

Here are some joint ventures I have set and run over the last few years. Each one is different and each had different challenges.

Rathmines St

My partner John and I purchased a property in our names and/or nominees. We initially formed a group and contributed cash for the purchase, intending to finance the build with development finance. However, when the COVID-19 pandemic hit, three initial investors withdrew, and we had to find replacements. If we hadn't been able to assemble a new investment group, John and I would have borne the risk.

Simpson St

I negotiated the purchase of the land and paid the deposit, always with the intention of forming a JV. People from the DevelopHer group expressed interest in taking one of the eight available positions. My approach was to be impartial,

(continued)

allowing first in best dressed to be involved. We did this by offering tickets that went live at a set time. With so much interest, within two minutes all the positions in the JV were taken. However, in hindsight, it might have been wiser to collate a shortlist and select participants that were more known to me. The situation was further complicated by having both a cash group and a borrowing group involved.

Clarke St

With a 10-day due-diligence period, I was under no pressure to finalise the deal. During this time, I assembled a group and obtained finance quotes, which was the low-risk and preferable option.

Jessie St

I purchased this property with an and/or nominee and finance clause of 10 days, providing me with security for 10 days work out the details. I used the cooling-off period and finance clause to ensure I had a group of investors for the project.

Structuring a JV

There are many options available for structuring JVs, but essentially the structure needs to work for whoever you have involved, what they will be doing, the length of the project and the way the capital is contributed.

The common ways we see JVs structured from a legal sense is as a JV partnership or a company structure.

I usually set up JVs to achieve a single goal — that is, renovating and selling a property. Other structures like companies and partnerships might be longer term and you might want to run a number of projects through them.

JV agreements

Ideally, you document your JV with a legally binding agreement that documents and governs the relationship between the people in the JV. This needs to be arranged by a suitable lawyer/solicitor and tailored to your individual situation.

Here are the key requirements you will need to decide on up front so you can prepare and draft your agreement:

— date

— party members

— contribution, both financial and in service

— the purpose of the JV

— division of profit and/or losses

— government and reporting

— dispute resolution

— term of the agreement

— exit strategies.

Consultants you will need to involve

While JVs can be amazing as they give you access to many more options than you might have alone, you will be working with other people and parties so it is important that you look to set these things up well to protect yourself.

Note that many of these consultants would be required whether you were running a JV or working on your own project:

— *Accountant.* It is important that you get both personal accounting advice in the best way to set up your share of the project, and advice on the best structure for the overall project.

— *Lawyer.* This will be to draft the agreement and protect your legal interests. Ideally everyone has their own independent lawyer, although in a practical sense this doesn't always happen.

— *Broker*. Depending on whether you need to borrow, a broker who understands borrowing for JVs will be really important. You will need someone who is experienced with both standard lending and development finance. The difference is in the fees, requirements, checks and balances.

Typical issues with JVs

You are working with other parties so you are introducing a number of different variables. Is this a problem? Not really, but it is something to be aware of. The shorter the term of the agreement, the less risk you will be exposed to — for example, you might understand what you are doing for the next 6 to 12 months so you can agree to work with someone for that period of time and if you decide you want to do something different over that period you could probably wait it out. However, if you are agreeing to work with someone over a 3-year period, there are many more twists and turns as well as family / life decisions that will be impacted by that agreement: you might have a baby, decide to move to a different country or want to invest in a business. We have less certainty as we project further into the future.

Here are some factors I would try to mitigate during the agreement phase:

— *Issues with fulfilment of contributions*. Can you rely on everyone to have the cash available that they are talking about?

— *Each party's understanding of what is 'fair'*. This seemingly simple term — 'fair' — is incredibly complex. You are working in a stressful environment. Are you comfortable that you will all feel okay with the agreement and the 'fairness' of the deal no matter what the outcome?

— *Change of circumstances: births, deaths, marriages*. People get sick, and bad things happen to good people on any ordinary day. What will happen if one of your JV partners has an issue?

— *What to do when things do not go to plan*. What if the renovation costs more than you predicted? What if the market flattens and you can't sell for a profit? I know you have run your numbers — after all, you have been through this book — but all investments are risky and not guaranteed to have a great outcome. You need to be able to work through the process with the parties you are investing with.

Are JVs right for you?

I see many people who love the idea of working on a JV project. I am not surprised. Personally, I do love them, but then sometimes I need a break. You are getting involved with a number of people and they all bring different joys, skills, complexities and adventures to your life. Table 4.3 (overleaf) sets out a list of questions for you to ponder before you go into one.

If you are looking to do a JV, then have a chat with people who might be interested in working with you. Drop it into the conversation that you are looking to do this type of thing and are looking for investors. If they are interested, they will follow up with questions — if not, they will just continue on with the conversation. Never try to coerce someone into doing a development with you: they are never a sure bet and can put a strain on your relationships, especially if one person feels like they were sold a concept.

And, before deciding whether JVs are right for you, reflect on the following questions:

— What is your ideal JV structure in terms of contributions? (For example, 50/50 cash and management with the other party, or you provide the property and they provide the cash? There are many set-ups but work out your ideal first.)

— Do you feel like another party would find this agreement fair?

— What track record do you have of making JVs work?

— Have you got an accountant and/or lawyer who can provide advice?

— What structures work best for you?

— Do you need to set up any entities or trusts, or get anything else in order?

— Do you need to complete any tax returns or understand your financial position more before doing a JV?

Table 4.3: Questions to ask yourself before embarking on a JV

Relationships and emotions	— Why do you want to do a JV?
	— What will it allow you to do that you couldn't otherwise?
	— When you think about how you work with others, what are your skills and weaknesses?
	— How will a JV mitigate some of the weaknesses and complement the skills?
	— What outcome do you need from the JV to make it worthwhile?
Investment	— What financial contribution would you be prepared to make?
	— What skills would you like to bring to the table?
	— How much time would you be happy to invest?
Your JV partners	— What gap (financial, skill, time) are you needing to fill by doing a JV?
	— Who would be suitable JV partners inside of your network?
	— Do you really want to work with them (think about on the worst day)?
	— How can you bring up this conversation with them without being pushy or selling them?
	— What would happen if something went wrong? Would you be breaking up a family or severing a friendship?

As I've said, I do love joint ventures and they have served a really great role and purpose in my early projects, helping me get started, and more recently as a way to bring groups of people together to leverage skills and invest in different types of projects. I have seen them work really well by allowing people to work together, pulling funds and time so they can jump in when they may not have otherwise been able to. Are they right for you? Only you can answer this.

Case Study: Working through a Joint Venture project

Working together with other parties in a Joint Venture can be a great way to run a project and pool funds. With teaching the process in mind we set up the BuildHer8 Joint Venture. The premise was that we could bring an investor group of seven women plus John and I together to build two beautiful, sustainably-responsible homes and have a lot of fun doing it. The original site had a planning permit for two large townhouses that didn't have great street appeal. The idea was that this project would be an experimental teaching project, one where we could demonstrate that developing with integrity and sustainable values would be well received by the community!

The seven women invested $200k each to partner with us. They were already within the BuildHer and DevelopHer community so they understood our values and the way we run our business, so when we spoke about the project they reached out to us to get involved. The premise was to set this project up as a play along JV, everyone in the investor group had a role to manage and to further gain experience in a different type of project.

We used local architects to design two houses, each with their own individualistic flair. The vision for each home was always to create distinct spaces that will speak to the homebuyers' sense of identity. This was done by using clean, fresh and contemporary lines, a sense of openness and an abundance of natural light. We softened this look with materials and finishes reflective of north-side style: sophistication and edginess served with a side of character and personality. The collaboration model lent itself to a unique opportunity for communal involvement, from planning and funding to design and construction.

(continued)

Originally two townhouses, the overarching value proposition of this Joint Venture was to reimagine the site as two independent homes with similar amenities but with different personalities. One house that was more sophisticated, darker and moodier and another that was light, bright, tonal and textural.

COVID was a major factor. Hitting in the settlement period, this was interesting to overcome with the investors as nerves around what was going to happen played out. This completely changed the way the build worked and flowed, with most of the build completed with only five trades on-site. We also had to work around supply chain issues that had become really common in the building industry at that moment. The team all worked exceeding hard to ensure that quality products and suppliers were used on the project, with many local suppliers favoured!

Building and living sustainably is becoming much more common and when building new homes and smart thinking in design can be easier to implement good decisions. Designing a home that could use renewable energy and was equipped with the right amenity to support it — like battery storage, electric car charging and heating and cooling systems — was front of mind for us. That, combined with the inherent benefits of good passive design principles designed into the heart of the building — such as orientation, natural ventilation and passive solar gain opportunities — were key factors in the concept design by the architects. Double glazing throughout with smart shading, under slab, ceiling and wall insulation helps the home perform better in fluctuating temperatures.

The result was that one house sold off-plan and the other went to auction. This all happened with the normal feels of developing. Jitters and debate about whether or not to sell, the price and some robust conversations formed the backdrop for this collaboration. The result was a return on the investors investment of 32.5 per cent and, as always, a lot of learnings.

Joint Ventures can be amazing ways to work as a team to develop and we love that in the BuildHer community we are now seeing our 'DevelopHers' come together to do their own JVs independently.

Remember, if you are looking to do a Joint Venture you will want to think about the following areas and how they will be managed before entering into an agreement:

— Due diligence. You will want to do some background checking on your partners if you do not know them well. Understand what they might bring to the party.

— Scope and roles. Make sure you document the objectives of the venture, the scope and the roles. Who will bring what to the table and how fair this is. There will be a mixture of time and money at play and the balance will need to be carefully considered.

— Determine the structure of the JV. What form will the JV take and how will it be founded? There are many types of JV and you will need to think about the legal and financial implications to find the best set-up for you.

— Dispute resolution and exit strategy. An agreement needs to be in place to unravel the JV if things start to go badly or someone needs to exit.

— Records and confidentiality need to be considered and determined. Deciding how this will happen adds to the clarity.

(continued)

- Personalities, cultural clashes and personal obligations. You will be working with this person or these people for a period of time so the more you can understand them and how they operate from the outset, the easier it will be.

- Seek expert advice to draw up the JV agreement and to set up the structures.

- Communication methodology. Determine how and when you will be communicating. What are the expectations of each of the parties?

A quick recap

— Managing cash flow is key to renovating and flipping property. Working through the budget and allocating funds is key to ensuring you don't hit any financial roadblocks or gaps beyond your contingency.

— Determine how much cash you need available for your build and how much you can borrow. Include deposits, renovation costs, holding costs, marketing and contingency.

— Calculate your borrowing power. You can do this by reducing debt, lowering expenses, increasing income or partnering.

— Finance pre-approvals enable you to bid at auction and transact with confidence so you can act quickly and with clarity.

— I recommend working closely with a broker who understands your goals to help you secure appropriate funding based on the lending environment and your individual circumstances.

— Products to consider when borrowing include offset accounts, equity releases, construction loans and substitution of equity.

— A good grasp on alternative financing strategies is also advantageous, including development finance and private investment.

— Joint ventures (JVs) are a way of collaborating and combining resources, possibly reducing risk. Ensure you have a JV agreement that clearly defines contributions, roles, dispute resolution and profit division.

Buying the right property: practical tips

I speak to so many people about their property dreams at BuildHer and during these conversations there is always a bit of disconnect at the point where they are looking to buy a property. There are really two pathways: learn first and buy after, or buy first and then learn.

The conversation I have with people will often unpack one of the following issues:

— If they don't have a property to work on, then it will be hard to learn as they need to have a property to renovate to be able to work through the process and how the numbers work.

— If they have already purchased, they are then running the numbers and scenarios on that property — hopefully they stack up. If not, then it creates a different issue: you will have a decision to make. Do you try to change what you are doing to create a product that does work, do you sell it as-is and take the loss or do you hold it for the long term?

The reality is, you are where you are and you can only learn from the point you are at. This is the real world and rarely is the real world black and white — or simple.

If you are buying a property for renovating, then the process will generally be:

1. Identify an area that you think will work as a renovation for profit.
2. Run some feasibilities to confirm that an area looks good, or you think you have a winner.
3. Get serious!

At this point I will assume you have found a property, run a feasibility on it, decided that this is the one, identified your scope of works and the numbers are working.

It's time to get serious and find out whether it really works and whether you'll be spending some cash!

The value of the property

People are often hung up on over- or under-paying for a property, which I understand. I think there are usually a few different values of a property, but ultimately, the value of a property is determined when it is sold. This means it doesn't have a fixed price but a variable one depending on who is in the market at that time and how much they are willing to pay for the property. And it is this lack of fixed price and certainty that drives people crazy.

From a pragmatic point of view, I usually look at the value of a property in two ways: the value in line with comparable case studies and the value the property has to me.

I can almost hear you asking, 'But why are they different?' Well, I have a market value, which is determined by looking at comparable properties that have sold in the area, how in demand they are, the features of this property when looking at those properties, the location in relationship to the comparable sales and the condition of the property. This is all clear. I touched on feasibility in chapter 2; however, I will explore this a little further in this chapter, and also include the value that this property has to you. The value that the property has to you needs to look at the general market value, but then also at what you can do with it alongside your projections.

Here's a silly example to illustrate the point.

What is the value of the property to you?

Say I am looking at a property and the comparable properties are sitting around $850 000. I know I could renovate this specific property and, due to access from an adjacent street and the planning regulations, I could do it for $500 000 (including all costs). After renovating and subdividing, I could have a block of land at the back worth $700 000 and the front block would be worth $1 500 000. So, I could sell the two properties for $2 200 000 at a cost of $1 350 000, meaning I would stand to make $850 000 in profit on this project.

Acquisition cost (based on comparable properties)	$850 000
Renovation cost	+ $500 000
Total cost (acquisition + renovation)	**$1 350 000**
Value of back block after renovation	$700 000
Value of front block after renovation	+ $1 500 000
Total value after renovation	**$2 200 000**
Total value after renovation	**$2 200 000**
Total cost (acquisition + renovation)	**– $1 350 000**
Profit	**$850 000**

The value to me is what I am prepared to pay to acquire the property. Let's say the project takes 12 months to complete and I am happy to make $500 000 out of this property in that time; then the value of this property to me might be $1 200 000.

This one works in that the property is worth more to me than anyone else, but conversely, another property might be worth less as it might not be worth my while to renovate it and put it back on the market.

You need to sense check the value of the property in the market in which it sits. However, I think it is really important to work out your walk-away point. And I determine the walk-away point as the point where I would not be annoyed with myself for not spending an extra $5000 to purchase the property. This number is based on running feasibilities and understanding my projected profits, but also the time, risk and cash investments I have sacrificed.

Purchasing property

You can purchase property in one of three ways: private sale or negotiation; at auction; or as an off-market deal.

Each of these types of purchases has its own unique quirks, in the same way that selling property does. If you are working in an area where you have a relationship with the local real estate agents, you may be able to purchase off-market properties, where the agent is able to broker a deal between the two parties. This means the vendor gets what they want and you, as the purchaser, can buy a property that fits your criteria without the pressure of an auction.

Private sale or negotiation

Private sales offer a more traditional route where the property is listed for a set price and you can negotiate directly with the seller or through their agent. This allows more room for negotiation, strategy and due diligence, and gives the purchaser a good indication of where they need to be sitting with their offers.

Pro tips

My tips for negotiating are to:

- *understand the seller's motivations (e.g. quick sale, highest price)*
- *use any market leverage to your advantage (e.g. buyer's market, timing)*
- *always have a clear maximum price in mind to avoid overcommitting.*

The timing of your offer can impact its reception. Consider approaching sellers just after an auction if the property didn't sell and is now listed with a set figure. Make sure you are aware of your timing and whether you are subject to auction conditions.

Unlike auctions, where the sale is unconditional, private sales allow you to easily include conditions such as subject to finance and building inspection. You will also generally have a 3-day cooling-off period during which you can exit the contract.

Purchasing at auction

Auctions can be highly competitive and fast-paced, often favoured for their transparency. Depending on the market you are in and the level of interest, they can still be a great way to purchase. You could be bidding against other purchasers so you will want to be prepared with your top dollar and understand all aspects of the property and your finance so you can bid with a clear mind. I have found that when you get wrapped up in the potential purchase of a home it helps to have your bidding strategies clear and preparations complete. You don't want to get emotionally wrapped up in the hype and over pay.

Bidding strategies

Bidding at an auction is an art form. There are many ways that people like to play the game. You will need to decide how you will play the game:

— Start strong or hold back? Explore different approaches to auction-day bidding.

— Read the room: Understand when competitors are near their limit.

— Take into account psychological aspects such as how to outmanoeuvre competitors without escalating prices unnecessarily.

With this in mind, I like to set my exit point before I begin. I always nominate a value that is not a round number. For example, I bid to

$1 310 000 on one property. It was to the dollar what I was willing to pay, but because I held strong and firm in my bids — always coming back with $5000 more straight away — it looked like I was in it until the end and the other potential purchaser dropped out.

Rules around auctions

Different states and different sales agencies have different rules around auctions and what you need to do. Some of them might require that you register your interest before they will accept a bid. Others might be on the market from when they begin, while others again might need to announce that they are on the market before they can bring down the hammer. Beware of the auction rules in your particular situation, but note the following:

— They are legally binding once the hammer falls, so it is important to have your finances and inspections sorted out beforehand.

— They are often cash sales, meaning there are no conditions attached (e.g. no subject to finance or inspection). There are some circumstances where you may be able to compete with a slightly different set of terms as long as you have had them agreed to by the agent and owner prior to proceeding.

Pre-auction offers

You may want to consider making a strong pre-auction offer to avoid the competitive environment of auction day, but by doing this you may also miss out on buying a very-well-priced project if no-one else is interested.

You need to understand when a pre-auction offer is appropriate and how to craft a compelling one.

Off-market deals

Off-market deals are often preferred by experienced investors because they provide the opportunity to secure a property without the stress of competition and being in the public eye. These deals typically arise from personal relationships with real estate agents who know the style of property that the purchaser is looking for and can approach them directly. Sometimes vendors don't want an auction because they prefer not to be in the public eye or to have the stress of presenting their homes and speaking to their neighbours.

Pro tips

— *Building relationships: Establishing trust and relationships with real estate agents and industry professionals is essential to securing off-market deals. Agents may reach out to you first if they know you're a serious buyer.*

— *Win-win approach: In off-market deals, both parties often benefit from avoiding the open market. The seller saves on marketing fees and auction pressures, while the buyer secures a property before it reaches the competitive market.*

— *Speed is essential: Off-market deals typically require quick decision making. Once you're offered an opportunity, you often need to act fast with due diligence to secure the property before it hits the market.*

— *Creative offers: In off-market deals, you may have more flexibility to get creative with your offers, including seller finance options, leases in the form of licensing agreements or even access for trades, depending on the seller's needs.*

Negotiating terms when purchasing property

People don't always realise that they can negotiate or attempt to negotiate on many items when purchasing a property. Buyers often focus on the purchase price, but there may be terms that you can negotiate to put you in a better position. You can negotiate to provide flexibility and align the purchase of this property with your specific needs or to mitigate risks. It's important to remember that while you can negotiate any terms you wish, the vendor has the right to accept or reject them. However, by negotiating effectively, you may be able to secure favourable conditions that protect your interests and may very well result in a win-win.

I'll run through some common items that are often negotiated in property transactions.

Purchase price

While the price is the most obvious item to negotiate, there are strategies you can use to influence how the final sale price is determined.

— *Offering below the asking price:* Buyers may start with a lower offer, especially if the market is slow or if they believe the property is overpriced.

— *Escalation clauses:* In a competitive market, you might include an escalation clause, where you agree to outbid competing offers up to a certain limit.

Deposit amount

The deposit is usually a percentage of the purchase price — often between 5 and 10 per cent, but this can be negotiated.

— *Lowering the deposit amount:* If your cash flow is limited, you may negotiate a lower deposit, freeing up more capital for other costs (such as building inspections or legal fees).

— *Higher deposit:* In some cases, offering a higher deposit might make your offer more attractive to the vendor and can show that you're a serious buyer.

Settlement period

The standard settlement period typically ranges from 30 to 90 days, but this can be negotiated depending on your needs and the vendor's circumstances.

— *Short settlement:* An earlier settlement might be desirable if you need to take possession quickly, but this may only work if the vendor is ready to vacate or the property is vacant.

— *Extended settlement:* If you need more time to organise finances or sell another property, you can negotiate an extended settlement period. This may appeal to vendors who are not in a rush to sell or who are looking to purchase and need time to buy the next property.

Subject to finance

This clause protects the buyer if they are unable to secure finance by a certain date. It gives you the option to back out of the deal if finance falls through.

By adding a finance clause, you can negotiate for a longer period to secure finance (e.g. 14 days instead of the standard 7 days) should you anticipate needing more time.

Conversely, an all-cash purchase might be a bargaining chip you can use to secure a property. If your offer is all cash, then the purchaser has more security than if you need to secure a loan.

Subject to building and pest inspection

This clause allows you to withdraw from the purchase if significant structural issues or pest infestations are discovered. You might need to look into the wording of these clauses to see what could or would constitute the right to withdraw from a contract.

— *Inspection period:* Negotiate a longer or shorter period for completing building and pest inspections.

- *Condition-based offers:* You can make the offer conditional on repairs being made if issues are discovered, or you may negotiate a price reduction instead of asking for repairs.

Subject to sale of existing property

If you need to sell your current home to finance the new purchase, this clause can protect you from being committed to two mortgages.

A subject-to-sale clause gives you the time needed to sell your current property. Vendors may not favour this clause unless they are also in no hurry to sell and you will usually have to put a value on the amount you are happy to sell your existing home for and a time frame in which you need to sell it.

Inclusions and exclusions

The buyer can negotiate what items will remain or be excluded from the sale.

- *Inclusions:* Common inclusions are fixtures such as light fittings, window coverings, appliances or even furniture. If you see something you like (e.g. a specific appliance or garden feature), you can ask for it to be included in the sale. I have seen things like furniture, TVs and fridges included in contracts. These items are all up for negotiation between parties, but be careful not to get stuck too much in the detail of the deal and overlook the greater property. In some cases I have seen inclusions such as building works (e.g. building a wall or fireplace, or fixing an issue that the purchaser wants) rectified before settlement.

- *Exclusions:* Similarly, the vendor may specify certain items they intend to take with them, such as outdoor features or specific fixtures. You can negotiate for them to leave these behind.

Early access

Early access allows the buyer to enter the property before settlement to start renovations or inspections. If the property is vacant and the owner allows it, you can also negotiate to put a licence agreement in place, which is the equivalent to a rental agreement for this specific situation.

I negotiate early access if I need to get access for our design team, land surveyor and geotechnical engineer so I can start our documentation and planning.

Some buyers may want to begin work early, especially if renovations are planned. Vendors may grant early access but generally there will need to be an agreement in place to cover what works are allowable during this time. And, as the purchaser does not own the property, it may need to be accompanied by an agreement to allow the purchaser to get building or planning approvals first.

Be aware that early access can be a liability issue, so it's important to clarify the terms and ensure adequate insurance is in place. Your conveyancer should be able to guide you here.

Rent-back agreements

In some cases, the vendor may need to remain in the property for a period after settlement, leading to a rent-back agreement.

— *Rent-back term:* If the seller wants to remain in the property for a while after settlement (e.g. if they're awaiting completion of their next home), you can negotiate a rental agreement where they pay you rent for that period.

— *Rental rate:* The rent-back terms, including the rate and duration, are entirely negotiable and should be formalised in the contract.

Special conditions

These are additional clauses that protect the buyer or vendor in specific circumstances.

— *Council approval for renovations:* You may want to include a clause that makes the purchase conditional on receiving council approval for planned renovations, extensions or on the purchaser's ability to lodge for approval during the settlement period.

— *Review of existing leases:* If you're purchasing a tenanted property, include a clause that allows you to review and approve the terms of the existing lease agreements before finalising the deal.

— *Subdivision or development approval:* If you plan to subdivide or develop the land, you can negotiate a clause that allows you to back out of the deal if planning permission is denied. This may also have stamp duty implications if the property is deemed to be developed between the purchase date and the settlement date.

Price adjustments based on valuation

This clause allows you to renegotiate the price if the bank's valuation of the property comes in lower than the agreed purchase price.

If the bank values the property below your offer price, you can include a price renegotiation clause that allows you to renegotiate or exit the contract without penalty.

Although clauses like this are unusual, especially in a rising market, they would be very helpful in the case where you needed to secure a loan and the valuation came in lower and you had to contribute additional funds to allow settlement to proceed.

Due diligence

This is the bit of the project where you are going to need to delve into the detail and make sure you are happy and comfortable with everything you are looking at. It's okay if there are issues with the property as long as they are discovered, addressed and factored into your equations. While not formally agreed, a due diligence period generally occurs before you purchase the property. It can be as little as a few hours where you are creating a plan and doing your research, or you can ask for a formal due diligence period as part of your offer, which means you commit to purchasing a property provided you're happy with the due diligence. This type of due diligence period would have an expiry date and is used to ratify an early stage feasibility, look into council requirements and make sure you are 100 per cent happy before you buy. All things you would always want to know before committing to purchase a property.

Location

The location of the property is as critical as the property itself. It influences the property's value, potential for growth and suitability for your project. One of my first properties taught me this lesson. I built a family home on a semi-main road with a bus stop out the front and carpark out the back. It made the street presence much better, but in doing so deleted a carpark, which was not a great market fit given its location.

There are many lessons to be learned on this journey and so often these are learned when we sell a property and assumptions or things that we overlooked become objections for purchasers.

When you start out, the property you can afford may sometimes be a less-than-ideal one, meaning it is discounted when you purchase it (making it more affordable) and it will most likely be discounted for the same reason when you sell it. There is nothing wrong with this, but when you are comparing sale prices it can feel disheartening. I like to consider it a stepping-stone property as it is rare to be able to purchase the perfect property in the first instance.

Neighbouring properties

Investigate the types of properties surrounding the one you're considering. Are they well-maintained, or is there a risk of living near neglected homes (which could affect the value of your investment)? Keep an eye out for future developments on nearby properties. Are the neighbours overlooking, or are there markers issues to come? Do they have 'No development' signs pinned to their fences?

Overlooking issues may be something you can overcome during the build process, so consider the impact on your plans now. Solving for overlooking by orientating an extension mass to the overlooking property can be a great way to increase the value of the home, but if you can't solve the issue, your sale price might be heavily discounted because of this same issue.

Try to think from a purchaser's perspective — for example, does the neighbouring property look like it has a hoarder living in it or perhaps a small group of university students? Is this where you would want to buy, or would that feel like a potential issue you don't want to take on?

From your own position, some neighbourhoods and neighbours can be a challenge to work with. Most of the time you will not know this until you build; however, if there are strong indicators, this may slow your progress. If you are looking to develop a heritage property that needs development approval or a planning permit and all of your neighbours have opposed development and have a reputation for blocking any works and hindering the progress, then this may place the property in the 'too hard' basket. I look to build and renovate with ease. Getting stuck in a fight or in planning can be really detrimental to your bottom line if your project is not one you can live in or has high holding costs.

Neighbourhood

Consider the overall vibe of the neighbourhood. Is it a desirable area? Are there signs of urban renewal, or is it a declining region? Look at the crime rates and demographic trends to ensure they align with your target market.

If you are buying and selling in a short period of time, don't be hoping for change or uplift in your neighbourhood. Rather, select your position carefully. Is it a good fit for the usage? In other words, if you are targeting a family purchaser and there is a brothel operating next door or a bus stopping on a busy road in front, then these are issues that your build alone can't overcome.

I once looked at a property that I really liked: a beautiful two-storey heritage home that seemed really well priced. With a bit of due diligence, I worked out that it was actually next to a brothel, which was why it was cost-effective. I hadn't noticed it on my first inspection. If something looks too good to be true there is often a reason for this!

Amenities

Proximity to schools, shops, parks and public transport can significantly influence the resale value of a property. Are there good schools nearby? Is there easy access to transport hubs or recreational facilities? It is so important to think like the end purchaser of your finished product. Will they want to live in this area? Some amenities being too close can be a hindrance. Is there a school next door that will cause issues with parking and school bells and limit the number of potential purchasers?

Train stations and trainlines can be positive and negative. Too close and it can be an issue of crime, security and noise, but as you move a few streets away, then great access to trainlines can be deemed a positive amenity.

Infrastructure

Check for any planned infrastructure projects (e.g. new roads, public transport extensions or utilities upgrades). While these can increase a property's value, construction work in the short term can disrupt your project.

I once built a property that had a trainline at the end of the road. During my build, as well as into the sales process, there was ongoing work in the street. They installed a wonderful bike path and vegetation, which significantly increased the streetscape appeal.

However, I sold before the work was completed so I was unable to benefit from these improvements.

In a market that is not rising rapidly, potential purchasers can be wary of taking on new issues and someone else's problem. Buying a home is a big deal, so building work and unknown projects and outcomes can affect the end sale price significantly. Conversely, I have seen properties increase significantly in value where access issues and infrastructure have been improved, but this can take a long time to come into fruition.

Planning schemes and future development

Investigate the local council's planning scheme. Are there any future developments planned that might impact the neighbourhood? These could range from large apartment complexes to commercial developments that may change the area's or property's appeal.

You can often have a look at the approvals at the local council office. It is common for people to sell a home they have held for a long period of time before a neighbouring property develops if they feel there will be an issue. I have seen this happen a number of times. Sometimes the property would have been adversely affected, but often it hasn't. A new home next door may be a positive for you if they have finished work before you are back on the market.

Property condition

The physical condition of the property you are looking at purchasing to renovate is paramount in determining the feasibility of a renovation project. I use a checklist to identify potential issues and the amount of work, and therefore cost, it would take to complete the works.

Here are some of the issues you should be looking out for when you are assessing a property.

Building foundations

Unsurprisingly, the foundation is critical to a property's long-term stability and if you have issues in this area they can be hard to overcome or rectify without significant work and cost.

Issues such as restumping can be common in older homes. If the foundation is unstable or lacks proper airflow, you could face significant and costly repairs. I tend to look for the condition of the subfloor and the overall access and ability to fix it. I'm happy to take on restumping of a property as long as there is enough clearance in the subfloor and surrounding ground to complete the work and prevent ongoing issues.

A dear friend recently showed me a home that they wanted to purchase. The timber subfloor needed work; the floor had rotted out and it felt uneven to walk across. The street level and garden areas were at the same level as the floor inside, which meant that first, we couldn't access the footings without cutting holes in the flooring inside, and second, the floor would have significant airflow issues and was non-compliant by today's building standards. There was no access to be able to assess the condition of the floor below, and this is an issue I would not want to take on as the rectification would mean removing all of the internal floors and subfloor structure and replacing everything that sat on top of it, including the kitchen and bathroom.

I don't tell you this story to scare you. However, if you are concerned, then getting advice from a builder, or someone who knows the process required to rectify the work, and factoring that into your costings, is important. If my friend was already planning to replace the bathroom, kitchen, flooring and the uplift to solve this problem in the property (potentially by pouring a slab or changing the substructure type), then this might not be an issue. In my friend's case, however, the renovation on the property was not that old and they did not want to do significant work as they were not planning to sell again.

Another home I purchased had terribly uneven floors. The walls were brick and the timber stumps and footings had moved. I was planning to replace all the flooring and there was plenty of clearance to complete the work in the subfloor. I was only keeping the front four rooms of this house, so in this case the issue did not bother me at all and I just factored rebuilding the foundations in that area into my costings.

Pro tip

A top tip here is to look for the cause of the issue. I have seen blocks with concrete yards that have sloped all the rainwater under the foundations of a house. Others I have seen have a significant flow of water towards a home and inadequate drainage or pest damage causing issues. First, identify the issue and then the cost to rectify the building works and the cause of the issue.

Necessary building work

Factor in all potential repairs to the property that do not form part of your renovation works. These could include:

— rewiring for electrical safety, or upgrading of services, to three-phase power

— roof repairs for older tiled roofs or ones that are clearly damaged, replacing guttering and downpipes

— insulation upgrades where a home might have none

— replumbing, especially in older homes where there may be issues with older clay pipes that tree roots can grow into

— window replacements if there are signs of rot and/or weatherproofing.

Ensure that these repairs are all budgeted for in your costings, and seek expert advice if necessary. Some costs are hidden but are necessary to get a good product at the end. We all like to factor in the fun jobs like replacing carpet or upgrading kitchens, but less fun are some of the building works that you need to do that don't change the perceived value of a home.

Our family home at the moment needs ceilings and light fixtures replaced, as well as replacement of the roof from tiles to Colorbond®, upgrade of the insulation, upgrade of the three heating and cooling systems to one unit, removal of gas tanks and replacement of all windows to higher performance ones. This work is expensive on a larger style home like this one and while a purchaser may notice new windows or the roof, these things all increase the comfort and liveability of the home but do not move the needle on the value because the home will look almost the same! When I renovate for profit, I really want the purchaser to see the value in the changes I am making and this usually means they can actually see the works rather than them being hidden in walls.

Pest infestations (termites)

Conduct a thorough pest inspection to check for any infestations, especially termites. Termite damage can be extensive and expensive to repair, and once fixed there can still be evidence that there has been an issue, which can be off-putting if a potential purchaser orders a building and pest inspection. If you are doing work on pests as part of your renovation, ensure any history of pest control is documented.

Water damage and drainage issues

Inspect for water damage, including leaks or mould. Check the roofing, basement and external walls for signs of past water issues, which can look like staining, bubbling paint, discoloration or areas that are coloured differently. Investigate whether the property is prone to flooding or water pooling, which could signal poor drainage. Poor drainage is often fixable, but drainage issues, rising damp and mould issues can again be expensive to rectify and this is often work that the end purchaser can't see you have undertaken.

If you suspect there could be an issue, get advice on how you might fix it and the cost you will need to allocate. Sometimes these issues are easily fixed but it means you are purchasing the home at a lower price point that significantly outweighs the cost of rectifying the issue because it scares away other purchasers. As always, it is about including the work into your feasibility rather than never buying a property with issues.

Garden and landscaping

Evaluate the condition of outdoor spaces and how difficult it would be to change them or to bring them in line with the newly renovated house. Is the garden well maintained or does it require significant investment? Look out for issues that will cost a lot to rectify, such as big drainage issues, underground tanks or huge amounts of concrete.

Some gardens and landscapes require little to make them sing, and others can be extensive and expensive. A long and large driveway in poor condition can be off-putting to a potential purchaser. If the only option is to upgrade the entire drive, is this going to be valued or is it feasible within your costings?

Sloping blocks and changing levels can be an amazing opportunity, but if you can't get access with machinery you need to consider how you will do the work cost-effectively and without using a lot of manpower.

Thinking about the external works and internal works from the beginning is really important. I see considerable uplift in value for properties that have a desirable garden. Zoning of external works and established gardens really helps to set your home in its surroundings. We have all seen newly completed builds with tiny and sparce plantings that feel like an afterthought. This is not ideal and will not make your potential purchaser feel like you care about the property.

Additional considerations

Every property has a different set of considerations depending on its style, size and location. You need to be smart and to consider all the work that needs doing and how much it will cost, but also the value and impact for an end purchaser. Here are just a few examples of the types of issues you may face:

- Units and apartments may have access issues to get building materials into the property and there might be a limit to what you can do inside the property due to the structure, which may affect apartments above and below yours.

- Sloping blocks can be amazing, or they can be hard to fix. Flow to external areas and navigating pathways might be a challenge, as might the loss of privacy due to being able to look into neighbours' properties. Conversely, there might be an amazing view due to these same factors.

- Large blocks and country properties can swallow your budget because of the scale of the external work.

- Small blocks with neighbouring properties on both sides might limit access and ease of building, but might also mean you run the risk of disturbing the footings of your neighbouring property. There may also be heritage requirements and restrictions to keep continuity of the properties that are adjoining.

Following are some other additional factors to think about.

Street presence and curb appeal

A property's street presence can significantly affect its future resale value. Consider the property's aesthetics and how it fits in with the neighbourhood. How can you make simple changes (like landscaping or painting) enhance its curb appeal? Be warned that sometimes the cute little unrenovated façades are as much work as, or more work than, the ugly ducklings. Are you overpaying because there is an emotional draw, or is the value fair and will that draw work for you when you sell?

I often see cute little single-fronted heritage homes in need of a renovation command a high price pre-renovation. It seems like an easy fix: a bit of paint and away we go! However, often these homes need as much work as the ugly one that has been stripped of its features because, among other things, you will still need to:

- replace the front window
- replace the verandah

- refinish the porch
- replace all of the boards at the front of the home
- replace the front door.

You can see that even though it is cute, to renovate it you will need to replace all the cuteness — but you are paying a premium for that emotional appeal. With the ugly one you will be doing all of the same work, but the buy-in price will have been lower, the transformation more dramatic and hopefully the uplift in value higher.

Sloping blocks

Is the block sloping? Will this mean that it is more expensive to build on? Have you factored access into the scenario? Sloping blocks can be hard to work with as they may require stairs or grading solutions. There may be issues with extending the property and creating a good connection to the landscape. Water runoff and falls become important, and often expensive as well. Personally, I love sloping blocks for the interest that they create, but they can be a challenge to work with from a building perspective as they create additional variables that need to be factored into the equation.

Orientation of the property

In the southern hemisphere the sun rises in the east and sets in the west. We are all taught this at school and we go about our days not thinking much of it. In building, the light, and access to light at different times of the day, is really important. People like light and bright properties. However, depending on the location, they may worry about the hot sun and heat loadings.

Always understand the orientation of your property. Where does the sun rise and where does it set? What does this mean for the rooms inside the house at different times of the day? Will this be a light-filled property or is the property going to feel dark? Which areas will have light issues and what can you do to overcome this? Are there any buildings or trees that will disrupt the amount of light you are getting? Is this an issue?

In Melbourne, people really prefer a north-facing back yard and in a lot of ways it does make life a lot easier with overshadowing restrictions if you are building up or extending. But no orientation is a no-go zone — more the orientation is just something to work around. In figure 5.1, you can see an example of how light will work throughout the day.

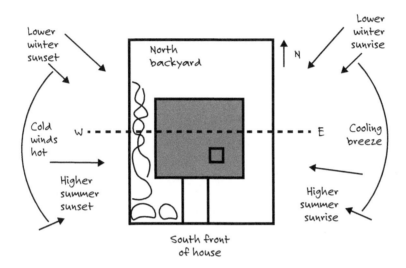

Figure 5.1: This is the sun rise and set during winter and summer on a house with a North facing backyard in Melbourne.

Existing permits

Have any permits already been obtained that might benefit your renovation (e.g. plans for an extension or subdivision)? Ensure that any permits are still valid and check whether you will need new permits for your work. Or are there any permits that haven't been completed, and that remain open?

One of our DevelopHers members, and mentors, purchased a property at an incredibly good price as there were works planned by the vendor that were unable to be completed and there was an open building permit. While, admittedly, it was a bit painful for them to go through the process of rectifying these issues, they purchased the property at a heavily discounted rate, which was a handsome payment for the increased paperwork.

Ownership of property

Make sure the seller is the legal owner of the property. Check for any co-owners, shared ownership or disputes that could complicate the transaction.

Your conveyancer should review the contract, but if there is a caveat over the property or there seem to be issues with the ownership make sure you understand the vendor's situation.

Easements and overlays

Some properties may have restrictions such as easements or overlays that limit what you can do with the land. You should be able to find this information in the documents that are provided with your contract of sale. Restrictions and limitations can include utility easements, heritage overlays or environmental protection regulations. Check the title first and then, if you are unclear, check in with the local council or authority to ensure you understand any limitations that could affect your plans and how you might work within the restrictions. Remember that they can't always provide detailed, property-specific advice.

If you need to renovate and sell a property quickly the red tape that these overlays and restrictions might provide could slow you down. They also might add additional costs for consultants, time and scope of building work that you will need to factor into your building price.

Service connections

Service connections include gas, electricity, sewer and NBN. Have a look at your property and ensure all of your required essential services are connected and in good working order. Different types of properties will have different connections. It is not uncommon for country properties not to have connections to sewers and to run from a septic pit. Inner-city residential blocks usually have connections for all of these services. There are recent changes to the laws around adding new connections for gas in many states of Australia. However, you may have an existing connection.

Here are some things to check:

- — Are water and sewerage lines adequate for any proposed extensions or additional bathrooms?
- — Are you connected to gas and do you wish or need to abolish this?
- — Are your powerlines above or below ground? Will you need to move or upgrade these?
- — Do you need to upgrade to three-phase power for large renovations?
- — Is the NBN or another high-speed internet service available?

Factor the cost of any upgrades to services into your feasibility.

Gut instinct

Pay attention to your intuition. Sometimes, despite the numbers stacking up, you may have a gut feeling that something isn't right. If you feel uneasy, consider walking away or seeking further advice before committing. I have looked at many houses that had good numbers but I didn't love them. They didn't speak to me and I struggled with feeling excited or enthused about the end result.

You will be spending a considerable chunk of time on this property and then at the end you need it to wow and excite someone else. If you are not excited, will your end purchaser be excited or is there something about it that means it doesn't speak to people and make them fall in love and want to make this their home? Only you will know the answer to this. Personally, I don't buy properties that are 'okay' — I want the excitement — and, from experience, whenever I have felt uneasy about doing something and done it anyway there have been challenges in the process that I might have been happier walking away from.

Finances

Obviously, before you even consider making an offer, it's vital to have a clear financial plan and realistic expectations regarding the property's potential profitability and, just as importantly, how you are going to cash flow the purchase and renovation. I know I have mentioned this often throughout the book, but the numbers are important and your access to cash is crucial to completing the project and not getting stuck in the middle. Explain how you will finance the build and project it to someone else, including the budgets along the way. Often, merely explaining and justifying will help you uncover issues.

Finance approval

Have you secured financing for the property, and do you think your lender will be satisfied with the valuation? Some lenders may devalue or only offer loan-to-value ratios on some properties at a lower rate — for example, instead of lending 80 per cent of the cost of the property, they may only lend 70 per cent. They may also discount properties that require significant work or are in unique areas. Some lenders will not fund a property that is land only or a bush block, so even though the numbers look amazing and you would make a healthy profit, your ability to access the cash is severely hindered. Check with your broker to make sure they think your plan is going to work.

Renovation funds

Double check your feasibility and ensure you have enough cash reserves or a method to be able to fund the renovation. Remember that unexpected costs can arise, so always allow a buffer for contingencies (10 to 20 per cent above your projected renovation costs).

Comparable sales

Check the recent sales of similar properties in the area. Do the sale prices align with your expected resale value after renovations? If the figures don't stack up, you may need to reassess the feasibility of the project. Have you actually checked the comparable sales or are you guessing? So often people guess rather than doing the work. If you don't have time to do the work before you buy the property, you probably don't have time to deal with errors in your assumptions at the tail end of the build either.

Market demand: sense check!

Are buyers actively seeking properties like the one you plan to create? Consult local agents to confirm demand, and check online platforms for market trends (e.g. how long similar properties remained on the market).

Feasibility review

Ensure you've run the project through a feasibility template, considering all costs, time frames and potential resale value. It's a good idea to have this reviewed by a professional (accountant, developer or property adviser) to ensure there's nothing you've missed.

Environmental and sustainability factors

Check whether there are any environmental concerns, such as proximity to bushfire zones or flood plains. Additionally, consider the existing property: will you need to implement energy-efficient solutions during the renovation (e.g. solar panels or double-glazed windows)? Are these requirements? Will they increase the property's value and appeal?

Structural engineer's report

For a property that you are concerned about, it may be worth investing in a building inspection or even a structural engineer's report to confirm the property's overall integrity, especially if you plan significant changes to the building structure or there are issues that you can't determine the extent of (like big cracks in brick walls, or underpinning that looks questionable). While it is expensive to get this done on a property you don't own, if you don't accurately allow time to rectify major structural works it could cause larger problems later in the project.

Historical significance

Some properties may have historical value and modifications may be restricted. If the property falls under heritage protection, obtaining permits and approval for renovations could take longer, be very expensive and require more investment. Compliance with heritage overlays may affect the bottom line considerably.

The value of your property based on comparative sales

Determining the value of a property based on comparable sales is one of the most reliable methods to understand whether you're paying the right price or setting a competitive selling price. Much better than trusting the real estate agent to tell you what it is worth! Comparable sales, often called 'comps', give you real data about how similar properties to the one you're evaluating in the same area have performed on the market. You will want to use this data to determine a price guide for the property you are purchasing or selling and as you are comparing properties you will also be able to analyse some of the market trends and features.

The idea of comparable sales is simple: properties with similar characteristics (such as size, condition and location) should sell for similar prices, and by tracking and analysing these sales, you can get a good sense of the current market value of your property.

Now, before you get too clever and dive into this topic, you really need to start by understanding what the value of a property actually is, which is the amount that a purchaser is willing to pay and a vendor is willing to sell for. These are not fixed prices and no two properties and purchasers are alike, so the price is subjective. However, this does not help us very much in our calculations: when we are trying to work out what the value is we need to be a little more analytical and try to understand the value proposition or offering from the purchaser's perspective.

Choosing suitable comparable properties to analyse

The key to an accurate property valuation is selecting the right comparable properties to use as your data points. Here's what you need to look for:

— *Location:* Keep your comps within the same suburb or, ideally, within a 1- to 2-kilometre radius of the property you're evaluating. Prices can vary significantly across neighbourhoods, so this helps maintain accuracy.

— *Size:* Compare properties with a similar land size and building area. A good rule of thumb is to keep the difference within 10 to 20 per cent of the subject property's land size, but as with anything, it will depend on your area and suburb.

— *Property type:* Houses should be compared with houses, and apartments with apartments. Ensure you're comparing like for like.

— *Condition:* If your property is unrenovated, compare it with other unrenovated properties. Similarly, compare recently renovated homes with each other.

— *Features:* Take into account features like the number of bedrooms and bathrooms, parking spaces, pools and other extras. Special features can increase the value, so you will need to adjust things accordingly.

Adjusting for differences

It's rare to find a perfect match, so you'll need to adjust the value of the comparable property to account for differences.

I do this by adding or subtracting from the purchase price depending on the differences. I always start by identifying whether a property is superior/inferior or similar on a spreadsheet and then I try to work out my subjective understanding of what difference this will make to the sale price. This is how I look to do this:

- *Size:* If the comparable property is larger or smaller by a significant amount you will need to account for this difference. One way might be to adjust the value based on the price per square metre. You can use a spreadsheet to calculate the average price per square metre of similar types of properties and then devise an assumed square-metre rate to adjust the value by. If there is a 20-square-metre difference on a 400-square-metre block, I would call this similar and not make any adjustments. The tolerance for differences will depend on your market.

- *Condition:* You really want to be comparing unrenovated properties with unrenovated properties as you are looking for the difference between a renovated and unrenovated property. But even so there will be adjustments to make. When you are looking at the property, think about whether it is superior, inferior or the same as others. Work out how much it would cost to bring your property to the same standard and subtract that from the comparison. Make an adjustment note based on this information. An example of this might be that your comparable property has a pool and your property does not, and the ones in your area with pools sell for around $200 000 more than the ones without. You might deduct the pool and therefore $200 000 from the comparable sale.

- *Location adjustments:* Even within a suburb, prices can vary based on proximity to amenities such as schools, transport or parks. There are super desirable streets that might fetch a few hundred thousand dollars more than the adjacent street, and then there are parts of streets that are sought after and others that are not. Properties closer to amenities may fetch a higher price, so make a note of such differences. I like to start with noting, again, whether they are inferior, similar or superior.

Now it's all well and good to sit at a computer making assumptions and taking notes, but there is no substitution for actually getting out in the street and looking at the properties. Agents are very good at presenting homes and can take images from the most flattering angles so you may not even notice that block of 40 apartments next door until you arrive at the property.

Finding comparable sales data

There are several ways to gather comparable sales data and compile it:

— *Real estate websites:* Websites such as *realestate.com.au*, *domain.com.au* and *onthehouse.com.au* offer recent sales data, including price, features and sale dates. This is the most convenient way to collect multiple data points and it is free and easy to do.

— *Agents:* Real estate agents are an excellent resource for recent sales. They often know of sales that haven't been widely reported and properties that were sold off market, and have insights into buyer feedback. You will want to build on this relationship and information once you have completed your first stage of research.

— *Websites such as corelogic.com.au:* You can compile all of this information into a spreadsheet like the one we use at BuildHer (see table 5.1, overleaf). Use this spreadsheet to start comparing properties. This allows you to organise and compare properties in a structured way.

— *BuildHer Collective*: We also have a program customised to allow you to get property data and insights quickly.

— You can download the spreadsheets and a free trial of our property at www.buildhercollective.com.au/renovate.

When I want to look at comparable sales, I log in to a real estate website — for example, *realestate.com.au*, which is free and readily available. I want to look at properties that have sold in the past 12 months (so, recently) but as the market has been a bit up and down I search over a longer period of time to look at any patterns. I then want to identify ones that have been new builds or high-end renovations to understand what the sale price for our Jessie St project will be. So I save them as 'favourites' to a search that is specific for this project.

When I save them like this, I can refer back to them at any time to see what inclusions and exclusions these properties have.

Table 5.1: Comparable properties analysis spreadsheet.

Property address	Price	Date	Reno /new build	m² of land	Size (inferior/ superior)	Beds	Bath	Car	Pool	Land- scaping	Finishes	Finishes (inferior/ superior)	Notes and comments
House 1													
House 2													
House 3													
House 4													
House 5													

In the case of Jessie St, there is a comparable property that sold recently for $4 700 000 and is similar in style and location to the property I am looking to build, which is lucky. Mostly, this will not be the case and you will need to make a more detailed analysis. I also like to map the properties according to location.

Are there specific locations that stand out above the rest? I really like to have a great knowledge of the streets and the areas that are more sought after — and other ones that might not be — in the suburb I am working in.

Once I have my comparable sales highlighted, I enter them into the comparable sales spreadsheet (see table 5.2, overleaf) so that I can review the data and look across the listings all together.

Visit www.buildhercollective.com.au/bookdownloads to download this or any other template provided in this book.

Analysing your comparable sales spreadsheet

It is one thing to gather the information and create the adjustments, but the gold comes from getting insights into what sold really well, how the purchasers felt about a property and how many purchasers there were at that level. As always, we want to start with the basics and adjust for the following factors:

— *Land size:* I calculate this the same way as for unrenovated properties, explained above.

— *Feature adjustments:* If a property has a pool and yours does not, adjust the price down to account for the difference. Similarly, if a property has a higher level of finishes or landscaping, factor in those differences.

Table 5.2: You can see from this completed table that I enter details, sizing and project information to create a range of sale prices for my project.

Property address	Price	Date	Reno /new build	m² of land	Size (inferior/ superior)	Beds	Bath	Car	Pool	Land-scaping	Finishes	Finishes (inferior/ superior)	Notes and comments
House 1	$4 100 000	2/03/2024	new build	600	same	4	3	3	yes	basic	good	same	Location of our house is better
House 2	$2 625 000	16/03/2024	new build	300	inferior	4	3	2	no	basic	excellent	same	Much smaller – beautiful build, land size was different
House 3	$2 850 000	27/02/2024	reno	446	inferior	4	2	1	no	nice	excellent	ok	Smaller, inferior location
House 4	$3 400 000	3/02/2024	reno	400	same	5	3	3	yes	basic	ok	inferior	Smaller block, inferior finishes, smaller house
House 5	$3 500 000	29/10/2023	reno	535	inferior	5	3	2	no	basic	excellent	ok	Older style, needs updating

— *Build quality*: This can be more subjective as it is based on your thoughts and feelings about the product you will be creating and how appealing it will be to purchasers. I might look at a property and, although it is in a good location, it is big and it has good features, it is not appealing because it has missed the mark of potential buyers from a style perspective. At the top end of the market, purchasers can be really selective as they have many more options.

— *Feedback:* Purchaser feedback can give you insights into what features drive demand. For example, if buyers loved the simplicity of one property's materials, you can consider that in your design or renovation decisions. The way you obtain this feedback is by asking the agent what has sold well, what people said about the house, what they liked and what they didn't like.

Common mistakes to avoid

As with anything, it's useful to know what to avoid doing.

— *Using outdated sales:* The property market can shift rapidly, so ensure your comps are recent (within the last 6 to 12 months). If they are similar types of sales, you might want to account for the changes in the market.

— *Ignoring condition:* Always account for differences in condition, especially with renovation properties, as comparing a fully renovated home with a fixer-upper without adjustments will skew the results. This means being critical and actually looking at it from the perspective of the purchaser, which can sometimes be hard to do.

— *Overvaluing unique features:* Not every buyer values things like a pool or high-end finishes, so make sure the adjustments for these features are realistic. Speak to a real estate agent about this to make sure they are seeing the value in the same things that you are. They are on the frontline.

— *Not considering the appeal*: Consider the floorplan, layout and styling of the property. You can learn a lot about what a market likes by where they spend their money.

I am always learning and growing, as is the market. Markets change and mature over time, and I am always on the lookout for properties that create competition. What is it that draws people in: what styles, what layouts? Are there materials or features that they want? Is there a commonality, or something we can learn by watching? The same goes for properties that are not well received.

I observed with interest one project that had the most stunning hero image of a kitchen. It was really striking and lovely. The property had masses of people visit and it was next to a park in a great location, but it really struggled to sell. You needed to delve deeper to work out what went wrong. The kitchen was beautiful but not practical. The butlers pantry had no benchtop power points. There was limited outdoor space as they had assumed everyone would use the park, but due to the location of the park there was also limited privacy in the home; and the landscaping felt undercooked and like an afterthought, which limited the curb appeal and meant people didn't feel the attachment or want to live there. All of these issues were easily fixed and certainly easy to learn from. It is a lot less painful to take learnings from someone else's project than your own.

Building and design codes

Each state and territory has a building and design code that guides the building surveyors and building certifiers as to what is acceptable and appropriate on a parcel of land. It's important that you understand the code in order to fast-track the process. Where there are no planning requirements that dictate otherwise, an understanding of your local code is absolutely advantageous.

Your knowledge of some of the key requirements can allow you to quickly and easily look at a site and determine whether there are any issues that would render it difficult to develop. The faster you can identify the site opportunities and suitability, the quicker you can work through whether or not this is a property that you are interested in working with.

Victoria

Victoria's codes and guidelines for residential development are called ResCode, and following are some of the key requirements that you should be aware of.

Site coverage

Typically, buildings can cover up to 60 per cent of the total site area, though this can vary based on local overlays.

Building height

For most residential zones, building heights are capped at 9 metres (two to three storeys), though higher limits may apply in growth zones.

Setbacks

Front setback: New developments must align with the average front setbacks of neighbouring properties.

Side and rear setbacks: As the height of the building increases, the setback from side and rear boundaries must also increase, starting from 1 to 1-and-a-half metres for single-storey buildings.

There are also setbacks relating to north-facing habitable rooms that dictate the adjacent property setbacks.

Private open space

Dwellings must have a minimum of 40 square metres of private open space for ground-level homes, with requirements for usability and dimensions.

Overshadowing

New developments must not excessively overshadow neighbouring properties' private open spaces, particularly in the morning and afternoon hours.

Overlooking

Measures must be taken to prevent direct views into neighbours' private open spaces or habitable rooms for a distance of 9 metres. Common solutions include screening, frosted windows or setting windows back.

Car parking

Developments typically require one space per one- or two-bedroom dwellings and two spaces per three or more bedroom dwellings.

Building on boundaries

Buildings can be constructed on the boundary line for a maximum of 10 metres in length and up to 3.6 metres in height, provided they do not adversely affect neighbouring properties (subject to local council variations).

• • •

There are many more requirements. When I assess a site for its suitability to purchase it as a project I find it helpful to understand how far back the front façade would need to be if I were doing a new build, or what my maximum site coverage is, or how much of the boundary I can build to. These guidelines give me a framework to design within to allow me to speed up and fast-track the process.

Each state or territory has its own set of codes and guidelines for residential development, much like ResCode in Victoria. Here's an overview of comparable regulations in other states.

New South Wales

In New South Wales, the State Environmental Planning Policy (Exempt and Complying Development Codes) 2008 — commonly known as the NSW Housing Code — governs residential development. This code allows for straightforward residential developments, without the need for a full development application, if they meet specific criteria.

Following are the key areas of the NSW Housing Code.

Building heights

Maximum heights vary by zoning but are typically around 8.5 metres for complying developments.

Setbacks

The minimum setbacks for front, side and rear boundaries vary but must be respected for building compliance.

Site coverage

Similarly to ResCode, there are limits on how much of the site can be covered by buildings (usually around 50 to 60 per cent).

Private open space

There are requirements for a minimum amount of open space for each dwelling.

Landscaping and environmental impacts

Standards for protecting vegetation and ensuring sustainable development apply.

Complying Development Certificates (CDC)

CDCs can be issued if the development complies with the rules, streamlining the approval process.

Queensland

The Queensland Development Code (QDC) governs all residential and other developments in Queensland. The QDC consolidates building requirements from various state legislation and provides specific standards for aspects of residential development.

Here are the key areas of the QDC.

Building setbacks

Similarly to other states, side and front setbacks are required to ensure separation between buildings.

Site coverage

Generally, the building footprint is limited to a percentage of the total site area (often 50 to 60 per cent).

Building height

There is a general limit of 8.5 metres, though this can vary by zone.

Privacy and overlooking

Rules apply about privacy between adjacent properties and overlooking, which may require screening or setbacks.

Car parking

Each dwelling must provide a minimum number of car parking spaces, typically one to two spaces per dwelling.

Western Australia (WA)

In Western Australia, the Residential Design Codes, commonly known as R-Codes, apply to all residential developments. The R-Codes are a comprehensive set of guidelines designed to control the density, design and layout of housing across the state.

Information about the key areas of the R-Codes follows.

Density

The R-Codes establish density codes (R20, R30, R40, and so on), which dictate the number of dwellings allowed on a given piece of land.

Building height

Restrictions vary by zoning but are generally 6 to 9 metres for standard residential developments.

Setbacks

There are specific setback requirements for front, side and rear boundaries, depending on the density of the development.

Private open space

There are requirements for each dwelling to have a minimum area of private open space, typically 20 to 30 square metres.

Car parking

Car parking spaces per dwelling are required, with different provisions for single-family homes and multi-residential developments.

Solar access and overshadowing

Provisions apply to ensure new developments do not excessively overshadow neighbouring properties.

South Australia

In South Australia, the Planning and Design Code applies to all developments, including residential. It consolidates the various planning rules and regulations into a single set of guidelines.

These are the key areas of the Planning and Design Code.

Building height

Similarly to other states, typical height limits for residential buildings are around 8.5 metres for single- and two-storey dwellings.

Setbacks

Requirements exist for front, side and rear setbacks to ensure adequate separation between buildings.

Private open space

There are minimum requirements for outdoor space, often linked to the size of the property or dwelling.

Environmental sustainability

Rules apply for energy efficiency, water management and protecting natural landscapes.

Character preservation

Specific guidelines exist to maintain the character of certain neighbourhoods, particularly in heritage or established residential areas.

Tasmania

The Tasmanian Planning Scheme is responsible for guiding residential and commercial developments across the state. Each local council applies the statewide guidelines, with some variations to meet local needs.

Here is some information on the key areas of the Tasmanian Planning Scheme.

Building heights

Maximum building heights vary depending on zoning but are generally 8.5 metres for residential dwellings.

Setbacks

Front, side and rear setback limits apply to maintain separation between properties.

Private open space

There is a required amount of open space, typically around 30 to 40 square metres for new dwellings.

Site coverage

Limits apply on how much of the lot can be covered by buildings, often 50 to 60 per cent.

Car parking

The minimum number of parking spaces required per dwelling is typically one to two spaces depending on the size of the house.

Northern Territory

The NT Planning Scheme sets out development controls in the Northern Territory, ensuring consistency in residential, commercial and other land-use developments.

The key areas of the NT Planning Scheme follow.

Building height

The height limit for residential buildings are generally 8.5 metres.

Setbacks

Prescribed setbacks ensure adequate separation between buildings for privacy and airflow.

Private open space

There are requirements for outdoor spaces associated with dwellings.

Car parking

Provision for off-street parking is mandated, typically one or two spaces per dwelling.

Australian Capital Territory (ACT)

In the ACT, the Territory Plan includes a Residential Design Code that regulates residential developments in Canberra and surrounding areas.

The code includes the following key areas.

Building height

Height limits apply for residential properties, typically 8.5 metres for most residential zones.

Setbacks

There are requirements for setbacks from front, side and rear boundaries.

Private open space

Minimum open space requirements apply for dwellings, depending on the size and location of the property.

Car parking

Typically, a minimum of one or two parking spaces is required per dwelling.

An expert buyer's advocate's thoughts on how to time the market

Amy Lunardi is one of my good friends, and an expert buyer's advocate who I know well and trust. She is the host of *The Australian Property Podcast* and creator of *The Property Guidebook*.

Amy works with many purchasers to buy their dream home or as a renovation for profit. We often talk about the market: what is happening in a broader sense and what is selling well, what is not and how the predictions are and are not coming to fruition. I asked her to comment on timing the market from a buyer's agent's perspective.

'I've been a buyer's agent for a decade, and not once have I heard a buyer say, "I think now is a really great time to buy a property". When the market is rising, buyers worry about overpaying. When it's falling, they worry that it'll fall even further.

'I'm not sure who coined the phrase "timing the market" but I can tell you one thing — nobody knows what the future holds.

'At the beginning of 2019, Australia's top property observers suggested price falls throughout the remainder of the year. A surprise election result and rate cuts meant that the exact opposite happened. When COVID arrived and it seemed the property market was doomed, the supply of property fell so sharply that prices boomed post-lockdown in Melbourne and Sydney. Nobody foresaw that.

'And if our top economists can't even get it right, what hope do you have in being able to figure it out? This becomes even more challenging if you're developing or renovating and you need to make decisions around anticipated future sale prices. In these instances, you should do your sums on

(continued)

today's numbers, not where you "think" prices might be in 6, 12 or 24 months' time when you're ready to sell.

'The way to approach a property purchase decision is to focus on things you can control and try to let go of things you can't. You can't control property prices, inflation, interest rates, government policies and stock levels. What you can control is figuring out if now is the right time to buy based on your own personal circumstances.

'These circumstances may include:

- Can you afford a property that ticks your "non-negotiable" boxes, in the locations you want? If not, what compromises are you open to making?

- How frequently are properties selling that you would consider buying? If there are a few sales a month you'd consider as "green lights", it's a promising sign that if you wait a little longer, you'll still be able to find what you want. If there's very few sales that suit, this either means your expectations don't align with reality, or what you're after is quite scarce and you'll need some patience.

- Do you have an adequate buffer left over once you buy?

- Are you prepared for further rate increases? How far have you stress tested your cash flows?

- Are you under any time pressure to buy (both from a financial and a personal perspective)? Sometimes pressure can be a good thing to help you make a decision; other times it can cloud your judgement if you feel like you're rushing into things.

- Will this property purchase achieve your goals and timelines?

- Are you on the same page as your partner?

- How long have you been looking for, and what's the reason you haven't had success so far?

— If developing, do the numbers stack up on today's figures, or are you relying on market growth to make them stack up?

'Once you're both emotionally and financially ready to buy a property, the right time to start looking is straight away. And then it's as simple as buying the right property (at the right price) when it comes up. I'm joking here — by no means is this a simple process. But being emotionally and financially ready will put you in the best position to be able to make a decision when the right property does come up for sale, rather than procrastinating or worrying about things that are entirely outside your control.'

A quick recap

— When buying a property for profit, it's essential to understand that the process isn't just about finding any property; it's about selecting the right one that aligns with your feasibility and renovation goals.

— Look at both the market value and the value the property holds specifically for your goals. A property might be worth more (or less) depending on what you can achieve with it.

— Properties can be bought via private sale, auction or off-market deals. Each has its unique quirks, with auctions being more competitive and off-market deals often benefitting those with strong industry relationships.

— Don't limit your negotiations to the purchase price. Explore other terms — like deposit amount, settlement period — and any clauses such as 'subject to finance' and 'subject to inspection' to protect your interests.

— Consider the local environment, neighbouring properties and potential developments. These factors can significantly impact the property's resale value and suitability for your project.

— Assess the foundational and structural aspects, existing permits and any necessary repairs. Major issues such as poor drainage, pest infestations or foundational instability should be factored into your budget.

— Review recent sales of similar properties to ensure your expected resale price aligns with the market. Accurately comparing properties ensures that your projections are realistic.

— Familiarise yourself with local building codes, setbacks and private open-space requirements to fast-track your project and avoid unnecessary delays.

— While numbers matter, trust your instincts. If something feels off about a property, it's worth reassessing before committing.

— Each property presents unique challenges and opportunities. Success comes from balancing hard numbers with an informed gut feeling, staying adaptable and keeping your end purchaser in mind from the outset.

6

Renovation: managing the design and build

While each project is different, here's the general process after you purchase or decide to renovate a property:

1. Design
2. Planning and approval
3. Tendering and budgeting
4. Construction
5. Handover.

After this, you will move on to styling and selling, if that's what you're intending to do.

I will give a brief overview of each of these stages and what will happen at each stage, but please remember that every build is different and will require you to look at your property and the work you are doing — and to choose your own pathway.

1. The design process

The design process can be complex or really straightforward — either way, it is incredibly rewarding when you nail your design! Getting the design right is fun.

Looking at the services you require from a designer, you will choose your design to fit with your feasibility and level of designer. Like most parts of the design process, you will need to work out where the value proposition for your build fits in. Your designer will set the tone and start to provide the communication that your trades will rely on. Your designer, under your guidance, will arguably have the greatest input in your final result.

If you are engaging a designer, it's important to find someone you connect with who you feel really understands your vision.

This is a big-picture stage. Be honest and open with your design team so that you can manage each other's expectations, both in terms of cost and of design.

The design process in a nutshell

1. Prepare a brief outlining the budget, key design guidelines and moments you would like to hit.
2. Illustrate the concept/schematic design, including the big-picture items such as floor space.
3. Develop the design, layering all the information so it will work for you.
4. Organise tender drawings, which are preparation documentation for builders (these may or may not be required depending on your needs).
5. Obtain stamped building permit documents.
6. Prepare on-site master construction drawings (these may layer in extra detail such as the interior design details).

2. The planning and approval process

The planning process protects you and your neighbours. There are many reasons you would need to go through the planning process, from heritage or building overlays to physical aspects of the land, such as its size. In the discovery phase of your feasibility you should have worked out whether you need to run through the planning and understood how long this will take.

The planning and approval process in a nutshell

1. Get hold of the title for your land and associated paperwork.
2. Source a feature survey of your land and the neighbouring properties.
3. Obtain relevant information from the council.
4. Prepare a design for the purposes of a planning permit or development approval.
5. Obtain a pre-planning application (a design review by a planning officer).
6. Organise a planning application — it's submission time!
7. Ask for a planning application and RFI (this will take 10 days, for a fast-track process, to several months, depending on your council and complexity of the build).
8. Receive the planning approval — stamped!

Names of approvals can vary state by state, so check in with your council.

Pro tip

Before you buy, make sure you reach out to the planning officer and ask questions. I hear you think, 'Eek! Ask the council?' Yes, they are there to help you navigate this process and 99 per cent of my dealings with them have been amazingly positive and informative. What would they be likely to support? What is a hard 'no'? Stay in touch politely to keep your planning application on track.

You can see how this process can add a lot of cost to a project — from professional fees including surveyor, arborists and traffic management documentation, as required, to interest costs while you hold a project.

3. The tendering and budgeting process

To make going out for tender as easy as possible for you, it's important to present all the information that clearly reflects the deal you are trying to do.

Best practice is to include a contract with your documentation to manage all expectations, including all delegated responsibilities, to prevent leaving anything to chance — and to minimise risk!

Include in your tender the timeline within which you would like to receive your quote, as well as a timeline for works.

Now, again, this will depend on the size of your renovation's scope of works and how you would like to work with the builder or trades. Certainly, you might tender out aspects of the build yourself or you might opt to do this yourself instead. Some areas that I find are helpful to get a read on costs are:

— floor finishes

— joinery and details

— stone and detailing

— windows.

The tendering and budgeting process in a nutshell

1. Organise tender drawings and specifications.
2. Request a quotation or tender document.
3. Raise a contract.
4. Allow time to quote properly (4 to 6 weeks).
5. Obtain a tender/quote analysis.
6. Find that combo of quality, cost and team!

---

4. The construction process

Mapping out the construction process can be a bit of a challenge if you are renovating and you don't know the process.

There is a slightly different process for a new build on an empty site: 'renovation (existing footprint and new extension)' and 'renovation (existing footprint only)'. The difference is nuanced and will depend on your design team and the lead you are taking, but it will generally travel along the following pathway. If your renovation, however, is retaining all of the walls and frames, then you will start from this point and proceed from there.

The construction process in a nutshell

1. Demolition
2. In grounds and foundation
3. Frame and lock-up
4. Fit-out and rough-ins
5. Finishing!

A basic understanding of these simple steps is all you need in the beginning, but you will need to know how to quantify each part of the process.

5. The handover process

Everyone's handover process will be different, but completion and inspection are, of course, a must to ensure you and your builder finish the job on the same page. Things do change throughout the build. Make sure you are satisfied with the finish you are given at the end of your build and don't be afraid of engaging in a few last-minute negotiations before making the final payment.

Remember to keep an open mind through the 'defects period': make notes, and send them through to your builder as a collective for them to address. Things happen!

The handover process in a nutshell

1. Complete building works.
2. Organise inspections.
3. Do your own inspection and create a defects list.
4. Arrange the final payment and negotiation.
5. Hand over or move in ('We did it, we did it!').

Your design team

Residential building has many levels of designers you might engage to help you work through your build and project.

You might engage design consultants such as architects, building designers, and interior designers and stylists. Or you might choose to manage the interior design yourself.

It is important to note that everyone in your design team can provide value in different ways and it is really up to you to find the value proposition in each when you look at the quality of work, the fees charged and the impact to the scope of work and levels of finishes.

Like most of your renovating for profit, you need to make value-based decisions on the property and what you are planning to do with it. In some circumstances, you might just be renovating and updating the interiors; alternatively, you might be doing a full architectural extension. I have run each of these methods on different projects for different reasons. It is important to pick the right fit — and to know the fit you need — to understand why you would use each design professional and what value they bring to the conversation.

Here's a run-down and some considerations on the various design consultants.

Architects

Architects are trained and accredited professionals who have studied for 6 years and then undertaken an accreditation process. They are top design professionals and have demonstrated their knowledge of spatial planning, material selection, form and the building process.

An architect will manage both the technical and the aesthetic and can generally provide an end-to-end solution, managing from concept phase to actually project managing the build. As with all aspects of a build, this is nuanced and subject to the actual architect and the practice you engage.

While the fees and costs can vary, in my experience you will pay between 5 and 10 per cent of the build cost for this level of service, but every practice and service you ask for is different. Depending on your requirements, the level of service you need and the documentation you require, you might ask for a different outcome. In my renovation/extension projects I often use an architect to the point of building permit drawings and I manage the design from this point forward.

Building designers

A building designer is, generally speaking, a more cost-effective option than an architect. The term has come to replace 'draftsperson' to more accurately reflect the role they play in housing developments. They are similar to architects, but with less extensive training. Building designers can be a great option to work with to keep the budget more manageable.

Your building designer may need to be registered depending on where you are located. They will need to complete their designs in accordance with local regulatory requirements for you to commence your build and will typically take you to the point of building approval.

Interior designers and interior stylists

It's a common misconception that interior designers and interior stylists provide the same service, but they have very different roles, different qualifications and work with different aspects of the build. There is a lot of overlap in this area of design depending on what you are asking for. Interior designers are specialists in the way things look and feel. They focus on the interiors of a home, providing advice on flow, materials, cabinetry, colour palettes, and fixtures and fittings. Interior designers can work externally from or alongside architects as part of the design team, depending on the size of the project and specialties of those specific professionals. If you don't feel comfortable pulling the look together, interior designers can be a great option for internal renovations and remodels within the existing walls of your home.

Interior stylists may only deal with the furniture and soft furnishings on a project. While you may engage a stylist for this role, it is more common on homes that will be lived in as the furniture will often be staged and removed, so it won't be required long term.

Self-managed interior design

Some of us are great at, and love, the process of design. We are happy to work out the kitchen layout or the paint colours and changes that we want to make in a renovation. If this is you and you don't need any regulatory documentation and sign-off, then you can do the design.

A huge part of doing the design is in your communication of that design to the build team, no matter which way you are building. This is the part that people often forget about when they are thinking about building and renovating. Communication is key and your clarity will be reflected in the pricing and smoothness of the build.

Before you take on the interior design, think about the complexity of the renovation and the methods you will be using to communicate with everyone. Will you be using schedules and hand sketches, or will you be documenting with a program like AutoCAD® or SketchUp®? There are times where each method would be appropriate. When I started, I would use simple sketches and schedules to manage the build. Now, on more complex homes, I prefer to have plans. It depends on your level of involvement and how much you can trust and rely on your build team.

Other consultants and professionals you may need

Other professionals you may have to engage include:

— *landscape architects and garden designers:* more and more the integration of the landscape and inside-out living is important. Connection to designed garden spaces and external living areas have been increasingly adding value to properties. You may need to look to do something yourself or you might look to hiring a professional. I have completed renovations where I prepared the design myself and where I have engaged designers.

— *structural engineers:* if you are completing structural works, removing walls or adding floor area, you will need a structural engineer to certify that the structure is designed and created correctly.

— *civil engineers:* a civil engineer may be required to look at the water and drainage and how you either retain this on-site or remove it from the site. It is less common in residential projects, but not unheard of.

— *energy consultants:* we need to build homes that are energy efficient.

— *geotechnical engineers:* these engineers soil test the site to inform the design team and structural engineer on the ground conditions.

— *land surveyors:* their job is to map out and measure the lay of your land prior to development.

— *town planners:* these professionals help with subdivisions, disputes and advice where neighbouring properties may be affected.

Choosing a building method

In this section I'll help you with identifying opportunities and obstacles, and choosing the right building method for you.

One of the biggest decisions you will make in terms of your time and your money is which building method to use.

There are many ways to run a project, but to generalise, these are the most common ones:

— owner-builder

— blended builder

— design and construct builder

— volume builder

— design and tender to an independent builder.

Each one can be great for a specific project, but they do need to align with your values, time and money constraints.

Let's break down the various renovation, construction or build methods — accepting that a new build might be the best result for your block.

Owner-builder

Owner-building is a construction method where the home owner takes on the role of the builder for their own residential project. This approach involves overseeing every aspect of the project, from design and planning to procurement of materials and construction management. It is important to know that when you are acting as an owner-builder you are assumed to have all of the same knowledge and therefore liability as a licensed builder. Table 6.1 (overleaf) reveals the pros and cons of being an owner-builder.

Table 6.1: The pros and cons of being an owner-builder

Pros	Cons
Cost savings: owner-building can potentially lead to cost savings as you can directly manage material purchases, negotiate deals and avoid builders' profit margins. You can shop around for pricing and change the materials as you go to pick up any specials. Often when people build like this they will build over time and manage their budgets and amount spent accordingly.	**Stress and responsibility:** the responsibility of managing the project can be overwhelming, leading to stress and potential mistakes. You will want to consider your tolerance and knowledge of building before you begin.
Control: you have complete control over the design, quality and execution of your project, ensuring that your vision is realised.	**Time-intensive:** owner-building demands a significant time commitment, as you'll need to manage various aspects of the project.
Learning opportunity: owner-building allows you to gain valuable insights into the construction process, enhancing your knowledge and skills.	**Limited expertise:** unless you have a background in construction, you may lack the expertise needed to navigate complex construction tasks. The biggest risk will be programming and understanding specific codes. You can rely on trades to help, but ultimately you will be responsible for the outcome.
Customisation: you can customise the project to your specific preferences, adjusting as you build if you need to, ensuring that your home truly reflects your personality and lifestyle. Sometimes this can help if you are struggling to visualise a space before the walls are all constructed.	**Permits and regulations:** ensuring compliance with local building codes, permits and regulations can be challenging without professional assistance. Again, trades can help, but if something major is overlooked it can be costly to rectify.
Flexibility: you have the flexibility to adjust the project schedule and make changes as needed throughout the construction process.	**Risk of cost overruns:** inexperience can lead to cost overruns due to unforeseen issues and mistakes during construction, or just lack of understanding on how to budget for a build project. There are many, many little costs that can add up over a project.

Cost implications

Owner-building can be cost-effective due to reduced builders' fees, but it's important to account for potential hidden costs, such as mistakes, delays and the need for professional consultations.

Time implications

Owner-building generally takes longer than hiring a professional builder, as you'll need to manage multiple tasks and coordinate with various trades. For a small project, if you are doing some of the work yourself you may, however, be able to manage it more quickly, as you are not relying on another party to schedule the work and the timelines.

Is owner-building right for you?

Consider these questions before embarking on an owner-building project:

— *Do you have construction knowledge?* Are you familiar with construction processes, codes and regulations?

— *Can you manage the project?* Do you have the time and organisational skills to oversee the entire project?

— *Are you comfortable with risk?* Are you prepared to handle unforeseen issues and potential mistakes during construction?

— *Do you have a support system?* Do you have access to experienced professionals for advice and guidance?

— *Can you balance quality and cost?* Are you able to balance cost savings with maintaining quality and safety?

Owner-building can be a rewarding experience for those who are well-prepared and have the time and dedication to manage a construction project. It offers control, customisation and potential cost savings, but it also requires significant effort, expertise and careful consideration of the associated risks. Consulting with professionals and creating a thorough plan are essential steps before embarking on an owner-building journey.

Blended builder

The blended builder method is a dynamic construction approach that combines the expertise of professional builders with the hands-on involvement of the homeowner. This method is designed to strike a balance between the convenience of hiring a builder and the desire to be actively engaged in the building process. Table 6.2 shows the pros and cons of being a blended builder.

Table 6.2: The pros and cons of being a blended builder

Pros	Cons
Expertise: benefit from the skills and experience of professional builders who handle complex tasks and ensure quality construction.	**Costs:** while costs can be more controlled compared to a traditional build, you will incur professional builder fees.
Collaboration: collaborate with a builder to bring your vision to life while tapping into their knowledge of construction best practices. This method allows you to work together to problem solve and resolve tricky details.	**Limited full control:** you may need to compromise on some design decisions to align with construction feasibility and best practices.
Control: maintain control over design decisions and project management while relying on experts for technical aspects. It does depend on how you structure this deal as to what control you will have: are you having them build to lock-up or are they taking ownership of everything except for some trades?	**Coordination:** effective coordination between the homeowner and the builder is essential, which can sometimes pose challenges.
Time-efficient: this method tends to be more time-efficient compared to owner-building, as professionals manage the critical stages.	**Hard to find:** not all builders will work in this way, so it can be harder to find the right builder and to negotiate your outcome.
Reduced stress: the division of tasks reduces the stress associated with full owner-building, allowing you to focus on creative aspects.	
Liability: depending on how you structure your project you might still be relying on a builder for all the warranties, which means that they will have insurance for this work and have ensured it is taken on correctly.	

Pros	Cons
	Reliance on relationship and documentation: the key to this method working really well is great documentation and a great relationship; if either of these are compromised then you can have a significant risk and it can be difficult to untangle.

Cost implications

The blended builder method involves professional builder fees, but these can be offset by potentially avoiding cost overruns and mistakes. You will still have control and the ability to pick up cost savings during the build process as there is more flexibility.

Time implications

The blended builder method typically requires less time compared to full owner-building, as professional builders manage critical aspects of construction.

Is the blended builder method right for you?

Consider these questions when contemplating the blended builder method:

— *Do you want expertise?* Are you seeking the expertise of professional builders while still being involved in the process?

— *Can you collaborate?* Are you comfortable collaborating and communicating with professionals to achieve your vision?

— *Do you value time?* Do you want a more streamlined process that saves time compared to full owner-building?

— *Are you open to compromise?* Are you willing to compromise on certain design aspects, or to work through details so all parties are happy, in order to ensure construction feasibility?

— *Can you manage costs?* Can you manage both builder fees and your budget to ensure cost-effectiveness?

The blended builder method offers a flexible and pragmatic approach for individuals who desire active participation in their project without shouldering the full burden of owner-building. It leverages the expertise of professional builders while maintaining engagement in the creative process. This method can provide a harmonious balance between creative control, time efficiency and construction expertise, resulting in a successful and satisfying building experience.

Design and construct builder

The design and construct (D&C) builder method is a comprehensive approach to construction that combines the design and building phases into a seamless process. This method involves hiring a single entity, a D&C builder, who is responsible for both the architectural design and the construction of your home. Table 6.3 breaks down the pros and cons of engaging a design and construct builder.

Table 6.3: The pros and cons of choosing a design and construct builder

Pros	Cons
Streamlined process: the design and construct builder method offers a streamlined process by integrating design and construction under one roof.	**Limited design independence:** while D&C builders prioritise collaboration, you may have less control over the selection of external architects and designers as often they will be in house. You may have issues achieving your desired design outcome if it is not aligned with the way the D&C builder likes to build.
Single point of contact: having a single entity responsible for both design and construction eliminates potential communication gaps between architects and builders.	**Dependency:** your reliance on the D&C builder's expertise can limit the scope for input from other professionals as they will typically manage the engineer, energy consultant and everyone else required through the design process.
Cost and time savings: the integrated approach can lead to cost and time savings as the builder is involved from the initial design phase.	Contractual complexities: complex contractual arrangements can be involved, which require thorough understanding and legal advice.

Pros	Cons
Efficient problem-solving: D&C builders can proactively address design and construction challenges, leading to more efficient problem-solving.	**Control of price and documents:** as you are designing with the builder (once you have all your desired inclusions) you might not own the documents needed to be able to undertake a price comparison. This can leave you locked into the build or starting over at the end of this process.
Design flexibility: collaborate closely with the D&C builder to customise the design according to your preferences and budget.	

Cost implications

The D&C builder method can potentially offer cost savings due to better cost control during the design phase and fewer communication breakdowns. However, you might get locked into a higher price by design creep through the process, and as there is no competitive tendering there are limited ways to control this outcome.

Time implications

The integrated design and construction approach can lead to a more efficient timeline due to fewer delays and smoother collaboration. However, this is still design, so it will depend on how quickly you can reach an agreement on the documentation.

Is the D&C builder method right for you?

Consider these questions when evaluating the D&C builder method:

— *Do you prefer streamlining?* Do you value a streamlined approach that combines design and construction?

— *Can you rely on a single entity?* Are you comfortable relying on a single D&C builder for both design and construction?

— *Do you want cost and time savings?* Are you seeking potential cost and time savings by involving the builder early in the design process? Can you manage the hiring process to ensure that you select a builder who will give you time and cost savings?

- *Are you open to design collaboration?* Are you willing to collaborate closely with the D&C builder for design customisation? And do you like the types of designs that the builder is presenting?
- *Can you navigate complex contracts?* Are you prepared to understand and navigate the complexities of contractual arrangements? Arguably, you will need to do this with any build, but in this case the one contract involves all of the professionals you would otherwise engage independently.

The D&C builder method is an efficient and collaborative approach that marries design creativity with practical construction expertise. This method suits individuals who prioritise a streamlined process, value single-point accountability and are open to close collaboration with a single entity. While relinquishing some design independence, the D&C builder method offers the advantage of integrated problem-solving, potential cost savings and a smoother timeline, resulting in a well-executed and personalised home build experience.

Volume builder

The volume builder method is a popular and convenient approach to home construction, offering pre-designed house plans and a streamlined building process. Volume builders construct a large number of homes each year, providing standardised options for various budgets and preferences. Table 6.4 shows the pros and cons of engaging a volume builder.

Table 6.4: The pros and cons of choosing a volume builder

Pros	Cons
Cost-efficient: volume builders leverage economies of scale, making their homes more cost-effective compared to custom designs.	**Limited customisation:** while volume builders offer various plans, customisation options are generally limited compared to custom builds and can have significant costs attached.
Potentially speedy construction: the streamlined process and standardised plans should result in faster construction timelines.	**Less unique:** the standardised designs may lack the unique character and personalised touches of a custom-designed home.

Pros	Cons
Reduced decision overload: volume builders offer curated selections, reducing the overwhelming choices homeowners might face.	**Location and site limitations:** volume builders often have predefined areas where they operate, limiting your choice of land. They may also have site limitations; that is, they will not build on a slope or a site with many trees.
Quality assurance: established volume builders often maintain stringent quality standards due to their consistent construction volume. You will want to check the build quality of the builder you are selecting in all cases.	**Less flexibility:** altering the design or layout may come with additional costs and restrictions.
Predictable costs: with fixed plans and specifications, you have a clearer understanding of the overall project cost.	**Only new homes:** you will not be able to use this process to do a renovation or extension — it is only for knock-down rebuilds.

Cost implications

Volume builders often provide cost-efficient options, but customisation or premium finishes could increase the overall project cost.

Time implications

The streamlined process and standardised plans could contribute to quicker construction timelines with volume builders.

Is the volume builder method right for you?

Assess these questions when considering the volume builder method:

— *Are you seeking affordability?* Do you prioritise a cost-efficient option without the complexities of a custom design?

— *Do you prefer a predictable timeline?* Is a potentially faster construction timeline important to you?

— *Is customisation less critical?* Are you comfortable with fewer customisation options in exchange for a simplified process?

— *Are you open to standardised plans?* Do you find value in choosing from pre-designed plans rather than starting from scratch?

— *Do you value quality and consistency?* Do you prioritise the reputation and quality assurance that established volume builders offer?

The volume builder method provides an accessible and streamlined approach to home construction, ideal for those seeking affordability, predictable timelines and simplified decision-making. While customisation options might be limited compared to custom designs, volume builders offer an attractive balance of cost-efficiency, quality assurance and faster construction. If you're looking for a well-constructed home without the complexity of a custom build, the volume builder method could be the perfect match for your new home.

Design team and tender to an independent builder method

The design team and tender method combines the expertise of a professional design team with the competitive pricing and tailored construction offered by independent builders. This approach provides you with a custom-designed home with the designer of your choice (architect or draftsperson) while maintaining cost control through the tender process. Table 6.5 explains the pros and cons of using the design team and tender method.

Table 6.5: The pros and cons of using the design team and tender method

Pros	Cons
Tailored design: collaborate with architects and designers to create a home that aligns with your unique vision and needs. If this is one of your values, then this might be a significant draw card!	**Design duration:** the design phase might take longer due to detailed customisation and decision making.
Expert guidance: benefit from the expertise of design professionals engaged by you who ensure your ideas are realised effectively.	**Tender complexity:** managing the tender process requires careful evaluation of bids and builder qualifications.

Pros	Cons
Competitive pricing: the tender process allows independent builders to submit quotes for your project, potentially leading to cost savings if managed well.	**Potential for budget variations:** while tenders offer competitive pricing, unexpected cost variations could arise during construction. The design process is also often unguided by price and you can be in for a big shock if expectations have not been set correctly.
Personalisation: you will work with designers to select every aspect of your home's layout, finishes and materials, ensuring they suit your values and preferences.	**Coordination challenges:** effective communication between design professionals, builders and you is crucial but can be complex.
Quality assurance: by selecting reputable independent builders through the tender process, you can ensure quality construction.	

Cost implications

The design team and tender method offers the potential for cost savings through competitive bids, but customisation and design complexity could impact the final cost. Essentially, the cost will be unknown until the tender is complete and then you may need to value engineer the process.

Time implications

The design phase might be longer due to starting with a blank slate and needing to engage and manage all the consultants. The tender process streamlines the builder selection process, but a good tender will take 8 to 12 weeks to complete.

Is the design team and tender method right for you?

Consider these questions when contemplating the design team and tender method:

— *Do you seek complete design control?* Are you looking for a home that reflects your unique lifestyle, preferences and needs?

- *Do you value selecting and assembling your team of consultants?* Are you willing to invest time in the design process to ensure your ideas are expertly translated?

- *Are you budget-conscious?* Do you want the benefits of competitive pricing while still maintaining customisation?

- *Can you manage complexity?* Are you prepared to navigate the tender process, evaluating builder bids and qualifications?

- *Do you prioritise quality?* Is selecting a reputable builder important to you to ensure quality construction?

The design team and tender method offers the best of both worlds: custom-designed living spaces and potential for competitive pricing (if this is one of the values you brief your team on). Collaborating with design professionals allows you to personalise every aspect of your home, and the tender process empowers you to select an independent builder who aligns with your vision and budget. While this approach requires careful management of design complexities and builder evaluations, the result is a home that perfectly captures your dreams while benefitting from expert guidance and cost control. If you're seeking a home that uniquely reflects you and your lifestyle, while also ensuring quality construction, the design team and tender method is a compelling choice.

The truly important thing here is matching your design team, build method and budget. Without taking this step you could be left exposed where you might have budgeted an 'owner-builder' budget that assumed you will not only let the trades do their thing, but you will also take on some of the works. Obviously, if you then take this budget and try to engage a high-end design and construct build team you will struggle to find anyone who can take on the project at this level.

The market may recognise that you have invested in a potentially higher quality of finish, but conversely you would need to revise your feasibility to ensure you remain on target.

How to choose the best builder and trades for you

Once you have worked out the delivery process for your build — that is, are you looking for a blended builder method, a volume builder, a typical builder, or a design and construct builder? — then it is time to select who you might like to work with on your project. Having a great fit in this area of the build is key to a successful process!

It is good to remember that you will be getting into a relationship that is both business and personal while spending a huge amount of money and trying to realise your dreams. With this in mind, you need to take the selection of a build partner or trades very seriously as it can make or break the project, particularly your experience of the project.

There is not always time to go through a huge vetting process with the trades, so look out for groups from which you can ask for referrals — for example, local mum's groups or area groups can be amazing. I have found some great contacts this way. Another way I have found people has been through specific building and renovating forums — for example, the BuildHer group. In fact, there are a number of builders who have been in constant work because they have looked after our members.

Here are some tips for selecting a builder or key trade to work with (especially with the view that you will want to do this again and again, so hiring well once will be time well invested!).

Understanding your brief

It is boring but true: you need to know what you are looking for, and the clearer you can be with your expectations and the way you want to run the project, the calmer you will be and the easier you will be to work with, which will make for a better process for everyone.

An example of understanding your requirements is to know whether you need a builder who can work alongside you on-site or one who will take control and get it done based on the complete documentation you provide. Either of these options is great; it's about understanding what you need and how you want to work within the team you are assembling.

Your budget will also need to match these expectations. If you are looking for a high-end builder who doesn't require any management by you, you will be looking at a certain type of business — potentially one with an admin team and systems and processes to support and facilitate this type of build — so the price that you budget needs to match.

It is important to make this clear here and now. Champagne taste on beer budget is not something that builders and trades like to hear. They want to do a great job for you and be paid accordingly. As a general rule, if they do less, you pay less, but there can be a big variance in the way builders and trades run their overheads and admin — which can vary the price a lot.

Researching your options

When looking for a builder, options are either plentiful or it can feel like they are booked for months in advance. As you have a good idea of what you are looking for, you can start asking for referrals from family, friends or neighbours who have completed similar projects to yours and have a brief chat with them to see if it looks like they will be a good fit or not.

I like referrals because you can understand the client's experience with the builder and make a shortlist. Another way I find builders is to literally drive around the area to see which builders are building locally. By driving around and looking at building sites, you can get a lot of information about how fast a site is moving, how clean the site is and whether this might be a builder you would like to add to the list.

As I'm sure you are aware, you can also search online for reviews and ratings of local builders and trades in your area, but I know this can be a little hit and miss. If you have recently purchased or have a good relationship with some real estate agents, they can also be a great source of information as they often know the locals!

You will be looking for builders you can work with easily. This means successful project completions and being able to manage things like time and budget.

Remember to keep a spreadsheet and notes. You can quickly forget who referred who and what their feedback was if you are not keeping track.

Checking credentials

Make sure the person or people you want to work with are licensed and insured to perform work in your area — do a simple ABN check and a builder registration check. Ensure they are using their own licence, and that they have completed this type of work before — or that you have confidence that they can do this type of work.

I always ask for examples of builders' past projects, references and testimonials from satisfied clients. Know that the referees you speak to will generally be provided by the builder, so they should be glowing. If you are still uncertain, you can always ask for a list of recently completed projects and addresses; you can drive by the sites that are still running and those that are completed and ask specifically to speak to owners of these properties.

Not all clients are amazing for builders and not all builders work well with clients. When you speak to the referees make sure you ask appropriate questions and read between the lines. Most often, people will give clues to issues without being straightforward if they have had issues.

Meeting in person and doing a site walk

For larger jobs, before tendering with a builder or hiring them to value manage the process, it is important to meet with them in person. Meeting in person will allow you to evaluate their experience and verbal skills as well as the non-verbal cues, like communication style and overall demeanour. Just like going on a first date, you will be assessing them, and they will be assessing you.

It's hard to keep perspective on this, but relationship fit is as important as pricing, and I would advise only asking for pricing from a builder who you would be happy to work with from a relationship standpoint. In other words, if you sense red flags and wouldn't hire them anyway, don't ask them to tender.

Before you tender is a good time to discuss your project in detail, ask questions about their past experience and expertise, and inquire about their availability and timeline. What type of projects do they want to take on and how might your project fit into their timeline?

I usually look to understand indicative costs and whether I think I can make them work within my budget, but I am also mindful not to push too hard here as the builder will need to do a detailed breakdown. When selecting a builder, I look for things like transparency and consistency in their communication and work processes. Your builder should be upfront about the progress of your project, any problems or delays that arise and how they are planning to resolve them. Communication should be effortless and frequent to ensure that you're kept informed every step of the way.

If it is difficult before you even layer in the pressure and stress of money and time frames, you can almost guarantee that this will not be an enjoyable experience.

Tendering and estimating

Obviously, your method of construction will determine how you run your tender and whether you select a particular builder to work with you to value manage the process.

If you are at the tendering stage with a builder and looking to get pricing from multiple builders, make sure you are transparent with your communication. Know the time frames and the expectation of when the tender will close and be awarded.

I like to maintain my integrity with my tenders and afford each builder the same opportunity. This is a process that you will want to manage carefully. It is one of the areas of the build I see people have the most trouble with, and as such, they have issues working out how to proceed when the quotes come back in. This is due to not setting up a generic tender response that the builders complete, which should help you to assess the builds.

I have a great module on tendering in the BuildHer course, but essentially you will want to think about this like a job that you are being paid to do and run it professionally. This means being clear in your communication, and providing complete documentation to all builders at the same time. You want to provide a tender submission spreadsheet for each builder to complete so you can compare your quotes easily, but understand that it will not be as easy as looking at the end dollar value. There will be some plusses and minuses in the quote. The more complex the job, the more detailed this analysis will become.

Tendering, estimating and quoting take a lot of time and are costly exercises for builders. These costs will ultimately be passed on to projects they build — so don't waste their time and money if you have no intention of using them.

Understanding construction timelines

Within the tender process, it's important to ask for a timeline of your renovation or build. You should already have an understanding of availability before you request a quote. Understanding the construction period will help you manage your own time and expectations throughout the process.

Make sure to communicate any deadlines or time constraints that you may have so that your builder can create a realistic and detailed timeline that works for both of you. Remember, you have spoken to past clients; if they have all reported that the build ran 2 months late, address this with the builder again at this stage. Understand what is realistic so you can plan, but also know the process that the builder works to.

When you are comparing builders, you will want to know if they are always on-site and committed to that one build. Or will they be moving across a number of sites, and will there be periods where no-one is working on your project? Expectations and understanding how they work is as important as the actual time frame. As are understanding expectations around liquidated damages and the cost to you if you are renting while the build is being undertaken.

Discussing the payment schedule

Alongside the overall price will come the payment schedule and an understanding of how you are paying for the project — that is, a bank loan with drawdown payments or cash, if you have it available. You will also want to understand that the builder has adequate funds to run the build and project. Building often requires out-of-pocket expenses for the builder upfront that are claimed back at each stage.

These are sometimes hard conversations to have, but if there are no issues, then they should be straightforward. The payment process and schedule should be clear from the outset.

Asking for the contract

When you decide to hire a builder, it is important to provide or ask for a detailed contract outlining all aspects of the project. This contract will confirm all timelines, materials and the full cost of the project. There will also be provisions and allowances for items supplied by the owner or not yet selected. Having a clear contract in place that references all of the tender documentation establishes expectations and keeps everyone on track. Ideally, you'll never have to refer to it to resolve issues, but it is there to protect both parties.

It is your project: keep yourself involved and stay organised

Throughout your build or renovation project, even if you have hired a builder to undertake all the work, it is important to keep yourself involved with the process and in constant communication with the builder to ensure that everything goes according to plan.

Provide feedback, ask questions and stay up to date with the progress of the project as much as possible. It may be a good idea to designate a main contact person in case any issues arise; this might be you or an architect or superintendent.

Organisation seems like a basic skill and something that everyone would do, but when things move quickly, believe me, you will want to have sorted this beforehand, so make sure you put all of the important documents in one place so they are easy to access.

I have a great Dropbox filing system that I use for builds so everything remains together and can be found easily. You don't want to end up in a situation where the lines of communication are blurred. So decide before you begin how you will manage your communication with the builder and set up a clear process that will be straightforward and easy for everyone to manage.

The building and renovating process

At this point of the build, you have planned and you have completed the design and sourced your team, so the time has finally come to get started on tearing down walls or laying the foundations to build on.

Congratulations: you have reached the fun bit! The bit that you were dreaming about from the beginning, before all the paperwork happened.

Understanding your construction process is going to be the key to getting through this both quickly and efficiently, staying one step ahead of your build team.

At this point, you have worked out if you are owner-building, blended building or hiring a builder. Regardless, you will need to stay ahead of the ordering and selecting if you haven't fully specified everything, to make sure the journey is as smooth and pain-free as possible.

This is the time where all that planning takes shape, where you can see your design come to life, where your organisation will either show you up or set you into a tail spin ...

Oh, right, there it is!

If you are running the project, selecting on the fly or haven't fully documented, then this, my friends, is the time when how well you budgeted, organised, pre-ordered and selected great builders and trades will come to fruition.

There may be moments where things become overwhelming, but remember this is why we did the numbers in the beginning. This is the part where you need to keep up to date with your ordering and costings because, remember, if you do this right it will be super fun and you will be wanting to do it again, and again, and again!

This is also the part where you will be building out those relationships with your trades or build team — the part where you get to learn, listen and take notes.

Who will you be working with again and who will you politely not use next time?

You will get to the point where you have a well-oiled build team, one you can trust and rely on to complete your projects. After all, networks and relationships are everything.

The process on-site

Outlining the build and renovation stages for an existing property is tricky because each project, and therefore each scope of works, is unique.

Some renos are confined to within the existing external walls and you may not need a building permit. For others that are more complex or require additional floor area — such as an extension up or out — you may have to build new and renovate at the same time.

If you are extending, then the general process is like a new build where you would lay the foundations, frame, clad, fit out and then fit off, but your first step will be to organise demolition of any redundant walls that are not needed in the new design, ensuring that the existing structure is propped up to support its weight. However, if you are renovating within existing external walls, then the process usually starts with internal demolition, moving or framing internal walls, and then running items like the plumbing and electrics.

While this might seem complex, it isn't really. It is just a process of what needs to be done when and which trades rely on others. Once you understand how you are building and the sequence, the rest of it will fall into place.

Pro tip

One of my top tips here is to have a site manager who knows what they are doing. There are things that can challenge a new renovator as trades rely on other trades to do work well and make allowances for the next one. For example, the carpentry trade needs to back block for any fixtures and fittings that will need to be fitted off, but their framing also needs to allow for plaster to be hung and fixed. This may mean straightening walls or putting furring channels across a ceiling to ensure it is level.

Will you be living in the reno?

Depending on whether you are living in the home you are renovating already or whether it is a site you have purpose purchased for renovating, you may be able to live in the site while you are building.

Be warned, this is a little like glamping, but it can also be stressful and exhausting. However, many of us don't have the luxury of residing elsewhere during a reno and our budgets depend on staging the work while we make do.

I have lived in many a renovation site and to be honest, most of the time I don't mind. But there are stages and times where it can get tricky and hard to keep up your buoyant happy outlook. It took me a number of projects before I reached the point where I could move out to renovate a house that I had lived in or do a project purely for profit without ever moving a stick of furniture in.

One project my partner and I lived in was tight on space and we had three children in this home. We staged the build so that we completed a master bedroom with ensuite bathroom before we knocked down the lean-to rear of the property.

Our makeshift kitchen was a trestle table in the lounge room, with a Thermomix, microwave, toaster and kettle. We had a BBQ outside and a fridge on the front verandah. I did find a note in my letterbox one day from a friendly neighbour asking if my fridge was still for sale — little did they know this was where it lived until the back of the house was locked up.

Most of our children have had a stint at having a bedroom that was to become, or was already, a walk-in robe, but honestly, I have such fond memories of making it work. Of getting through it and the sheer joy at another area being finished as the house was built around us.

This may or may not be appropriate for you. This may or may not work with your family, but for us we were able to save money on renting another house. We were able to stage the work so we could close off areas and by being on-site at all times, there is an urgency, push and sense of adventure that we wouldn't have otherwise had.

By living on-site, you know when tradespeople are coming and going, and how the team is working together, and can immediately sense if something is not quite right. Living on-site can allow you to workshop and solve countless issues that might come up and can give builders, contractors or trades an inherent sense of accountability working alongside you. It is also so much easier (and faster) to answer those pesky questions that crop up along the way if you are always available. You can easily pick up elements that don't adhere to your plans, such as incorrectly placed walls and windows, or monitor the tile set out to make sure it is perfect.

I find that living on-site, or at least within 5 minutes of the site, is incredibly helpful. It is not an obvious benefit of living in a renovation, but travelling to and from your site is time consuming! I learned on one of my projects that was 15 minutes away off peak and 30 mins on peak that this travel can fast become a burden if you are working fulltime or renovating around kids and commitments.

If the site is just 30 minutes from where you live, it is an hour round trip every time you visit. I like to be on-site at least twice a week — it's too exciting not to be! — so this would mean adding an additional 2 hours to your week, just for travel. You also then need to time your visits to coincide with trades and if you are meeting people for quoting they are often late, and this can be a pain. That's where my 5-minute rule came from (which I talked about in chapter 1) — all the projects were in one suburb, which had the additional bonus of meaning I became a suburb expert.

There are obviously also many problems that stem from living in the renovation ... from dust, to substandard living conditions, to safety, to insurance. It may or may not be a possibility. Not only that but some builders will not build with you on-site. If you are staging the work, then this can take longer and you will have a lack of privacy with people coming and going.

To be clear, my preference is not to live among a renovation, especially with children; however, honestly, I am often not that bothered — it just depends on the end game, the stage of the project and how much I am doing at any one time.

In short, budgets can be tight at the beginning of your journey and living in can be a huge cost saving and allow staging of finances in a way that might not be accomplished otherwise.

Pro tips

If you are going to live in, I have some tips for you:

— *Do whatever you can to prepare for dust. Try to block up the entry to the renovation as best you can and seal the openings. This may not be convenient if you want to constantly keep an eye on progress, but it will give you and your family some privacy and help keep the renovation where it is meant to be.*

— *Remind yourself why you are living the way you are and keep an eye on the end result (it will help when things get frustrating).*

— *Pack up everything you don't need in sealed containers. Living in a reno is a great way to practise preparing*

(continued)

for an overseas trip. Take only what you need — for example, if you are renovating in summer, pack away your winter clothing.

— *Once you get closer to a finished home, a shoes-off rule will really help! Outside there might be mud and mess, and a constant supply of little rocks, which are very easily walked into the house.*

— *Demaroato the renovation into zones and think about what you need to do and when. Completing an ensuite before the rest of the works, for example, will give you access to a bathroom for the remainder of the renovation, but it can also mean living in the renovation for longer.*

— *Finally, have a sense of humour and be grateful! In the grand scheme of things, the disruption will only last for a short period of time and the end result will feel even more luxurious and lovely after a little bit of 'camping' in your own home.*

Honestly, having done this myself and having watched other people do it I can say that no matter how long the build, it seems that our sense of humour and our patience frays with about 2 weeks of construction to go. When you hit this point, try to remember to have a sense of humour and look at the big picture. It is a privilege to get to do what we do, and, honestly, just like childbirth, you will not remember this time in 6 months' time!

A quick recap

— Every renovation journey progresses through five stages —
design, planning and approval, tendering and budgeting,
construction, and handover. Understanding each of these
stages and what needs to happen ahead of time ensures
a smooth process.

— Assemble the right mix of professionals — architects,
building designers, interior stylists, structural engineers,
and more — based on your project's requirements
according to your brief, budget and preferred way
of working.

— There are various building methods: owner-builder,
blended builder, design and construct, volume builder, or
design and tender. Align your method with your budget,
values and desired level of involvement.

— Evaluate your builders and trades through referrals,
credentials and in-person meetings. This may be
a relationship that you have for a long time, so
choose wisely.

— Renovating is a blend of vision, preparation and
adaptability. By mastering these stages, you can bring
your dream project to life with confidence and control.

Selling your property: an overview of the sales process

According to *realestate.com.au*, the average length of a sale campaign is 21 to 30 days, but the highest level of interest is shown in the first 10 to 14 days. You need to have a clear game plan about how you will sell your property, who will sell it for you and what it is going to cost.

When you're thinking about renovating for profit, you want to maximise your return, so focusing on each area of the process, understanding it and then leveraging it to get the best result possible is of great importance.

Prepare your property for sale

This is a complete topic on its own. There is no single guide on how to best prepare your property. Rather, you will want to read the market, looking specifically at your market and analysing the best method for you. This will typically involve a listing, and an agent who can guide you through the process. However, I have found the more I understand and am in control of the process and the many different options available, the better I can manoeuvre myself and adjust my expectations to get the best result.

If you would like to choose who helps you prepare your property for sale, you will find this list of people typically needed when selling a property helpful.

— *The vendor*. That's you! At this point you have led the project all the way through, and I would expect this to continue being the case.

— *The agent*. Your agent will generally have the biggest role to play in the sales process. This is why they are in business: to sell houses. They should provide a strategy and an understanding of what they will be doing from the outset. They usually are paid a percentage of the overall sale price.

— *An auctioneer*. If you have selected to sell by auction you will need an auctioneer; this may or may not be the agent.

— *A photographer*. In most markets, certainly inner-city markets, you will use a professional real estate photographer to take images for your listings.

— *A floorplan drawer*. You may wish to get a stylised floorplan drawn of your project so you can list your home on the online platforms.

— *A copywriter*. They will write the words around your marketing campaign.

— *A styling company*. They provide real estate styling for your project, which is particularly helpful if you are not living in the home that is going to sale because, to display it in its best light, you will want it furnished.

— *The conveyancer*. They will undertake the legal side of the property transaction, from the sale to the settlement.

— *The lender*. If you have finance on your property you will need to involve the bank to settle your project.

- *Building and pest inspectors.* Purchasers might wish to undertake a building and/or pest inspection. Sometimes it might be useful to know a company that can be relied on to refer potential purchasers to.

- *A vendor's advocate.* If you do not feel comfortable with the process, you might wish to use a vendor's advocate. They will be independently hired by you, but will generally be paid by commission split with the agent. They will help you get your property ready for market by helping guide the styling, selecting the agent and sales process, and running point on the negotiation process with the agent.

- *Buyer's advocate.* The purchaser might have a buyer's advocate who is negotiating on their behalf.

Market and sell your property

There are several steps involved in the sales process, from getting the property ready, to having it on the market, to settling the sale. You'll want to know the various sales strategies and options available, compare your property to other similar ones on the market, select an agent, style your property and market it correctly.

I'll deep dive into all of these aspects later in this chapter — but first, here's an overview of preparing to be on the market and settlement.

Getting ready to be on the market

This incorporates finishing your project, creating a plan, selecting your team, getting comfortable with the process and working with everyone to ensure you have the best result. Most people focus on this as it is the bit they can see.

In the lead-up to getting ready for market, you will want to plan ahead and book in the following:

- Real estate stylist
- Real estate agent and campaign dates

- — Photographer
- — Conveyancer (start readying your documentation)
- — Sign-offs — that is, occupancy permit or Statement of Compliance
- — Marketing of your property.

On-the-market to sale date

Ahh, this bit! Keep up momentum and make sure your property shines as much as possible — go for it on the marketing front if you can. Make sure you thank everyone for their hard-earned push! If you haven't already, put together all the things a new owner might need: warranties, instructions and some notes on your home.

Also, take this time to finalise your numbers. Assuming you may have become a touch busy during the completion of the project, it is a great time to do a bit of analysis on how your project went. Finalise your numbers, note what could have been organised earlier, what you might do differently next time and what worked really well, and gather a list of trades you would work with again to put into a document.

Get your eye back in the game. How does your home compare to others? Can you tweak anything? What is the market feedback? I like to adjust the order of the online images of my property weekly to make it a little more fresh when people are scrolling through. Take note of what the agent is telling you and know that many agents will use this time to adjust your expectations down. This will make them look much better when they come to you with an offer and will also make closing the gap between expectation and offer easier if there is a difference.

Settlement period

Speak to your conveyancer about the type of contract you have and potential cooling-off period. Often, private sales processes, along with expression-of-interest campaigns, have a three-day cooling-off period — so don't celebrate too early — whereas an auction campaign doesn't afford the purchaser the same privilege. Are there any conditions in the contract, such as building or pest inspections, or perhaps a finance clause? Your conveyancer is best placed to explain the contract and the different levers within.

Pro tip

If your mortgage is below a certain level, you can often apply to the other party for a release of the deposit that has been paid. This can be really helpful to start to reduce any debt, or to leverage yourself into purchasing another property, as it can be the deposit. Talk to your conveyancer in the preparation period of the contract about how this works. You will need to apply to the bank to get a current loan value, and generally meet some other conditions.

Settlement day

The person who has purchased your property will generally be entitled to a pre-settlement inspection. This can be a bit of a shock to them because the furniture has been removed and the property is stripped back to its bare bones. I make sure it is clean and as nice as possible for this day.

On settlement day, I like to leave a note and a bunch of flowers, or something to say that I care about the home. This is a house I have toiled over for countless hours, and I really want the first impression to be amazing.

• • •

So, is marketing and selling your property a fun process?

Umm, sometimes — if people are lining up at the door. If all the research and marketing has been done and there are many people fighting over your property! If the market is rising and there is a healthy sense of FOMO. If you have run your numbers and there is a great profit no matter what happens.

The reality is, the project keeps you busy in the lead-up to it being on the market. There is a big build-up to finishing and launching and then it is photographed, sent out into the world and there is not much you can do about it after that. The decisions have been made, you have put your best foot forward and you are awaiting the day of judgement in the form of an offer. Everyone likes different parts of a build, but I would be lying if I said this was the bit that I like the best.

Either way, enjoy the process if you can. Learn from feedback, get out there and start planning your next property, if you haven't already purchased one, and use all the information you gather to get better at your craft. Doing one project is great, but it is the continuation of doing project after project that will bring you success over a period of time and allow you to really hone your skills.

Let's now look at some of the key decisions and stages in the sales process that you can control to give you an edge over the other houses on the market. Don't get complacent in the last mile!

Common sales strategies and processes

There are several ways to sell a property, including the following more common methods.

Off-market

An off-market property sale is where you list your property with a real estate agent. They take it to the purchasers on their database, along with any buyer's advocates, to see if they have a potential buyer for your property without doing a full marketing campaign.

Private sale

This is where the property is advertised for private sale, either with or without a fixed price. The buyer and seller agree on a sale price through negotiation, usually with the assistance of an agent.

Auction

An auction is led by an auctioneer, who is hired on behalf of the vendor. There are a few different ways to run an auction, but in general purchasers compete on an open market via bids and, as long as the final bid is above the vendor's reserve, it will be sold to the highest bidder.

Expressions of interest (EOI)

If you want to market a property without a price, but with a closing deadline, you can market it by EOI. Buyers are encouraged to submit the best and final offers, but the control really is with the vendor as they will receive all the offers and can then decide which way they want to go.

Off the plan

An off-the-plan sales contract is an agreement to sell land before either a subdivision or construction has been completed. There are reasons this could work for the purchaser and/or the vendor, but there are a few complexities that you need to be aware of when you enter into an agreement like this.

Your agent will generally have a preference for one or another type of sales process depending on where you are selling and they will generally also have an accepted way of selling the property. Regardless of these details, have a think about what you are selling and why you would like to take it to the market one way or another way.

Ultimately, you have your agent as a guide, but you can control the method of sale to make sure you are comfortable.

I once sold a house that was a bit different from any of the houses that were on the market at the time. I decided to take it to auction as I had had a good experience with the auction process, but as it got closer to the day I knew that I didn't have a great buyer pool. I did, however, have one stand-out purchaser who saw more value in the property than the other lukewarm purchasers.

I decided to proceed to auction because of this potential purchaser, but really, in hindsight, there was no other active party ready to push this buyer. Because of that, once the property was on the market I was only going to achieve marginally over the second bidder's bid.

When the auction reached a halfway mark, I needed to make a decision to put the property on the market or to pull it off. The smart play would have been to pull it off and negotiate directly with the one keen purchaser, but I chose to put it on the market. In the heat of the moment, in the fluster of action, I chose to proceed, hoping maybe for a hail Mary or secret bidder to materialise from nowhere. It sold at $5000 above the vendor's bid, which was actually a good result, but what wasn't was the way I played the game. If I had pulled it off the market I may have been able to come closer to the purchaser's top dollar, which was $240 000 above what they paid for it.

How did I know this? The purchaser was using a buyer's agent and they gloated to me afterwards about what they were authorised to spend to acquire the property. First of all, this is really not nice. Second, that $240 000 would make a nice addition to my bank account to this day.

What did I learn? Some properties are different or unique and they don't have a lot of, or any, comparable sales. Some of these properties are really difficult to value and the value that one purchaser sees is different from what the next purchaser might see in the property. Even though auction is one of the most common methods of sale, it is one of a number of methods that you have available to you in your toolkit.

Market conditions

The state of the market at the time you are ready to sell can significantly influence the success of your sale. In a hot market, an auction might drive competition and push up the price. FOMO and great buyer sentiment can give buoyancy to the right product, allowing for multiple players to push their limits.

However, in a cooler market, you might want to consider having a private sale or off-market approach. This will target serious buyers without the pressure of a public auction if sentiment is down and there are fewer purchases playing at this time. An off-market, or pre-market, campaign can be particularly helpful to sound out the market and see what the reaction is. Some agents like to introduce a few key purchasers who are in the market for your product before the listing goes live in a VIP sense. This can give you valuable insights.

I like to run a full marketing campaign in most cases. My homes are designed to have good hero images, and I try to be unique. But catering to a broad market and a public campaign will be your best way to maximise eyeballs and interest, and ultimately to get some purchasers through the door by creating competition.

Understanding the market dynamics — whether it's a seller's market or a buyer's market — can help you choose a method that aligns with the current climate and will help to get your expectations set at a realistic level.

Look at your competition on the market

It seems obvious, but really it may not occur to you, to check out your competition in the thick of your preparations. Before deciding on a sales method, take a good look at what else is available and ask the agents what they have already listed and what is coming to market. Are there similar properties to yours currently listed? If so, how are they being marketed? The way your competition is selling can give you valuable insights into how to position your property. If similar homes are going to auction, it might be wise to follow suit, but if they are passing in at the auctions, or are sitting on the market for longer than normal, perhaps a different approach is needed.

The funny thing about real estate is that so much of it is driven by sentiment, which can change in a week. There will still be purchasers in a nervous market, as there are in a rising market, but the feelings they have and their willingness to push themselves might be different — all with the same basic inputs. There may be no change in the amount of money they earn, their lending capacity, your product and their need for a new home, but the fear of missing out or of the market moving again can be enough to get an extra push.

Your job in choosing the right campaign method is to assess the market, understand what it is seeing and then work out which method of sale you think will be able to draw out the best purchase price and leave you least exposed.

Goals and time frames

Everyone is in a rush to sell at the end of the project. Loans always need repaying and now that you've finished your project you need to move on with your life! Understanding the implication of each sales method in time is really, really important. Bringing the purchasers to a date of decision by auction or closing an expression of interest can be a great way to try to reach an outcome. Do speak to your real estate agent about the pros and cons and the average sale time in your market to understand if you are being realistic or not.

Your agent should provide insight into how you should sell your property. A good agent will run you through the pros and cons and make a recommendation based on their experience. As they sell hundreds of properties, they should be best placed to guide you in the direction that will bring you the best outcome aligned with your goals.

Critical review: compare your property with others

At this point I want you to compare your property to other similar properties that have sold recently and the ones that are on the market. Fill out a spreadsheet like the one in table 7.1 to help you look at your current situation from a less emotional viewpoint.

Table 7.1: Spreadsheet for comparing properties

Property address	Price	Date	Reno/ new build	m² of house	Size (inferior/ superior)	Beds	Bath	Car	Pool	Land-scaping	Finishes	Finishes (inferior/ superior)	Notes and comments
House 1	$4 100 000	2/03/2024	new build	0	same	4	3	3	yes	basic	good	same	Location of our house is better
House 2	$2 625 000	16/03/2024	new build	0	Inferior	4	3	2	no	basic	excellent	same	Much smaller – beautiful build, land size was different
House 3	$2 850 000	27/02/2024	reno	0	Same	4	2	1	no	nice	ok	ok	Smaller, inferior location
House 4	$3 400 000	3/02/2024	reno	0	Inferior	5	3	3	yes	basic	excellent	Inferior	Smaller block, inferior finishes, smaller house
House 5	3 500 000	29/10/2023	reno	0		5	3	2	no	basic	excellent	ok	Older style, needs updating

The expected sale-price range based on the amounts in table 7.1 is:

Minimum	$3 900 000
Average	$4 300 000
High	$4 500 000

Use table 7.1 to see the actual sales figures of comparable properties and whether they are inferior or superior. We all have hopes and dreams about what we will get and, fingers crossed, that we are able to achieve an amazing price. But, to accept an amazing price you need to know that it is an amazing price in the first place, which will only happen when you do the work to understand what is selling in the market now.

This spreadsheet should be familiar. I used it in chapter 5, in the feasibility section of the process, to see what I could sell for. I was using hypothetical information about what I would be able to achieve and since I first completed this table I would imagine there have been a few more sales and there are a few more properties on the market.

Set your expectations in line with reality to understand what you should be doing as a vendor. Remember, what you have spent on the house is irrelevant to the purchaser — if you have overcapitalised, this exercise will be hard for you. As much as possible, you want to look at the house from the viewpoint of the person who is buying your home. Can you see what their options are and how your property compares from an impartial vantage point? Understanding this will really help you work out your pricing strategy.

Setting your sales price

There are laws that govern what you can and cannot do in terms of the price you list a home for. Different states, and markets within them, have different processes and also standard practices. Listen to the advice you are given, see how your property will be positioned with the current stock on the market and also do your own research. Make sure you completely understand the pricing strategy that will be part of the real estate agent's presentation.

What happens if it doesn't sell?

You do need to consider this outcome and have a back-up plan. How long should you keep it on the market, how likely is this to happen and what are your options? The options generally include relisting at another time, changing agency, changing your pricing strategy, changing the way you sell the property and bring it to market, and withdrawing it from the market.

This can be so tricky to navigate, but you need to have a property that will perform well for you and sometimes the best option is to cut and run. If this is you, hold your head up high. There are always going to be new experiences, and learning when to accept something and move on to the next one is part of the game.

Select and work with an agent

When I select and work with an agent I really like to work alongside them in a way that means we are both getting the most out of the relationship. Remember that your goal is to build long-term relationships that will benefit you into the future.

I like to start working with an agent early on in our planning piece, as I explained earlier in the book, for various reasons.

Partnering with the person who is going to be selling your property and who is connecting with the market on a daily basis really helps to create the best product possible. I look to get insider information with regard to what people want, what they are saying and how they are reacting to other properties.

Critically, you need to have started this relationship early to understand the agent's perspective on your plans. Things like three good bedrooms vs four smaller rooms — which is better? Or, do I need a study? Or, how are people reacting to X or Y about the property?

As you progress, you will want to get insights early about similar campaigns. Is there something purchasers are going wild for — for example, a double-sided fireplace? Or are they 'ho hum' in reaction to certain features? One that comes up a bit is the market's appetite for colour and playfulness in a home — is that good and does it stand out? Or is it a challenge to sell? Different markets are... well... different. So is the level of execution, to be honest.

One of the key things I look for in this relationship is the ability to have uncomfortable conversations at the right time. Like, 'Look, I think you need to up your game here' or 'The market isn't supporting those numbers — you need to list lower'. Talking about hard things is, frankly, really hard. I have had many of these conversations with one of the key agents I have worked with over the years: uncomfortable moments where one party was being brutally honest in a kind and caring way, but in a way that wasn't what the other wanted to hear. The truth will stand and our relationship is better for it. You grow as a team when you work together.

Choosing the right agent

Needless to say, it is so important to select the right agent. They are your voice, your spokesperson about your home and the one who will convey to the market all the little details that make this home perfect. They are the one on the frontline negotiating with the purchasers and introducing passive parties to the campaign.

Red flags include, 'A good house will sell itself ...'

Early on in my renovating career I made some really, really big blunders with homes I had created more for myself than for the market. When I was selecting the agent for this campaign I went with one who had called and followed up with me for a few years. When I was listing the property, I had interviewed two agents. I was actually about to select an alternative agent, but when I spoke to him about not proceeding he wrote me an exceedingly long text criticising every aspect of the other agent: telling me how the house would sell itself and that he had put the work into listing our home. The other agent apparently had not, in his eyes, earned this listing. As a 20-something I felt pressured and I caved listing with the agent who had canned all the other agents in the area and had essentially demanded that I owed him the listing.

Overpromising and not having had hard conversations was the way this relationship went. We did get plenty of people to the opens. It presented well, but it was not the right product for our market, with six bedrooms, limited yard space and a smallish kitchen. There were many things I would do differently if I was renovating this home again, but one of the major issues could have been dealt with easily. In fact, six weeks after the campaign, significantly under the expected price point, I turned two of the rooms into a large second living area to be able to get a deal done. The agent also dropped his commission in this transaction to ensure it got over the line with me and the purchasers. From my perspective, I agreed to sell below what I was expecting, to move forward on my adventures rather than continue to battle to achieve a higher price point.

With this experience, I purchased another home and was determined to do it differently. Thankfully, I am very into learning from my mistakes. As I was coming up to the end of the next build, this agent resurfaced. As I believe honesty is the best policy — and I also have a memory like a sieve so I would find it hard to keep a story straight — I told said agent that I had decided to list with a different agent.

The response? I was sent another very, very long, very rude message. I was informed that I may never purchase from this agent (though I imagine purchasing at an auction would be hard to stop). He informed me that he would not show me through a property that he had co-listed — one that I would have been the best purchaser for — which I ultimately purchased through the co-agent. As I was taken aback by this response, thinking perhaps it was a badly constructed joke, I turned up at an open home that weekend only to be told that 'I had made my bed, now I need to lie in it'.

Now, I understand that there are many times when an agent might feel disappointed in some vendors or potential vendors' actions. I am sure they often have every right to be, but the long and short of it is that they act for the party whose house they are selling. If they refuse to speak to the best potential purchaser or refuse to allow a potential purchaser to buy from them because they are harbouring a personal vendetta, then this is not acting in good faith for their client.

I have heard many stories of a similar ilk, so I would say choose wisely which agent you list with and look at their behaviour over a period of time, preferably before they court you to sell your home.

This leads me to the question, 'How are you going to select the right agent, especially when working in a new market where you don't know who any of the agents are or whether they can be trusted'? It will take a bit of time, but I would not make the decision based on what a friend says. The truth here is that we tend to have confirmation bias: we love people to do what we do! Ever asked someone about the school their child is in? They almost always have to say it's great because they send their loved and cherished babies there day after day!

Okay, let's move on... what should you look for in an agent?

Professional reputation

I want to know what the professional reputation is of an agent in an area. You can start by looking online and seeing how many listings they have had in the past year. There are many online sites that will track this information and exchange it for selling your details to the agents in the area. I would tend to look at the online listing platforms for this information as they will have the most current and less biased results.

Look for:

— the types of properties they are selling and the associated prices they are fetching

— how many properties they are lead agent for — that is, market share

— reviews from sellers

— their recently sold properties.

Local market knowledge

I like to test local market knowledge in person. When I am doing my secret shopper rounds of properties that are similar to those I want to sell, I will ask what similar properties have been on the market, how long they have taken to sell, and what were the good and bad aspects of the location. A brief chat, but one where I am leaning on them for information, not proving how much I know. Are there any upcoming or off-markets we can look at?

Track record experience

You want to look at the properties that the agent has had for sale in your category.

How long were these houses on the market? If I am looking to sell an apartment that I have recently renovated, then I would like to work with an agent who sells apartments in this area. The reason is, I want my agent to have connections with purchasers of this type of property. If they always sell apartments, then at every open they will meet people who are looking at apartments, so their list of contacts will be the type of people who would be looking to buy my product.

Marketing savvy

This one is always subjective and will depend a little on the properties, but have a look at how the agents present their listings, both when you look at them in person or online. Have a read of the property information. Does it make sense? Are there any glaring issues that speak to attention to detail? Are you drawn in by the photography? Are you taken on a journey through the home on the online listing? Are there marketing brochures and communications? Have you joined their list and are they emailing you potential property matches? Do they have a social media account? Are they actively promoting the properties they have for sale?

Communication

In my earlier days, one lovely agent would not look at me when I spoke to him. He preferred to address and speak only to my partner, John. No matter how hard I tried (it became a game) I could not get him to engage with me. Now, yes we were both looking together, but I can tell you I didn't want to talk to him much about properties, and I'm a pretty open person. I would have let him know our budget, what we wanted and that we were looking for a purchase in the next month.

Think critically about the agents you speak to. Do they return your calls? Are they listening to you? Will they give you the time of day before they know you have a property to sell? As a potential purchaser, I want to know how you feel.

One of the best agents I work with, I don't speak to a lot while I have a property on the market. I get an update and report but I don't spend a lot of time analysing the potential purchasers unless there is a decision to be made. An agent basically has their time and connections to work a sale. If, as a vendor, you are taking a lot of the agent's time — using them as a counsellor to settle your nerves while you are on the market, trying to get the agent to commit to what price they will be getting a sale at — you are wasting their time, and this is time when they are working for you!

An agent should have all the time they need for purchasers, and be effective and concise when dealing with vendors. Ultimately, they get paid when the deal is done and settled — so let them do what they are good at: getting deals over the line.

Negotiation skills

I like to try to get a sense of an agent's negotiation skills. Do I trust them? Do I think they will negotiate hard on my behalf? If I have purchased from them I would have a sense of this, but it is hard to test without this. One of the few negotiations you have is around their commission and whether they will fight for this.

Compatibility and rapport

This comes down to trust, and whether you think you can work with a particular agent. Real estate agents often have a bad name. They are coined as sleezy. I do wonder whether, culturally, Australians have an issue with sales and the sales process.

Do you prefer a direct style? Will the agent work with you on this? Are they clear in what they tell you or are they just mirroring your thoughts? Are they interested in you, but are they also sharing a bit about themselves?

Connection in the community

Is the agent connected within the community they are selling in?

Incidental conversations and moments of connection in a local area are gold and ones that as a vendor and purchaser I would want to tap into. Let's say the agent is at school pick-up and invests time into getting to know the people there. As a result they know that Joan is renovating her home and wants to sell it when she's finished. This gives them a few insights that they can work with: there will be a renovated property on the market and Joan will need to find somewhere to live.

Now, if they are having these conversations in and around the area all the time they can start to make connections. For example, Ben from the soccer club has had enough of trying to get his plans approved and he would actually prefer a finished home; Tim from the coffee shop has been chatting too and he is looking at moving out of the suburb when he retires and will be selling his home to travel around Australia.

The community is where the action is happening. To be honest, it would be tiring being an agent who works in a local area because you would want to be across everything that is happening — births, deaths, marriages, divorces — as these are the times when people are searching for a new place to live and you can help to introduce more passive purchasers to the market.

The team around the agent

Does your agent have a team? 'Are they selling alone or in a team?' is a key question to ask. An agent's job is to list properties and to sell properties, but there is so, so much more to an agent's role than this! They have to send contracts, organise for properties to be online, organise access for building inspections and coordinate marketing. In my experience, if you have an agent who is busy and is good at the selling aspect of the process they may not be amazing at the paperwork aspect, and this is where a team can come in handy.

If your agent has a team, try to understand this structure. Who is manning the opens? Who will be doing the call-backs? Who will be your support through the campaign?

How do you test some of the above aspects before selecting an agent? You will be working with an agent, not an agency, so you need to be comfortable with the individual. I have found the hiring of an agent can often be a popularity contest: who you like best and who you think you will get along with best.

Deciding between agents

If you are deciding between agents I would encourage you to take the following steps and ask these questions to compare them:

— Who has the listings that are similar to what you are selling online?

— How are they marketing their homes?

— Visit open homes — be a purchaser. Do they give you the attention and have the discussions you would want to have with an agent?

— Will they negotiate their fee? Do they fight for it?

— Do you feel like they work hard for the sale or are they complacent?

— Do they have interesting insights about properties?

— When you speak to them about your property, are they prepared for their session with you or not? Have they done their homework?

— How do they communicate with you?

— How do they speak about other people, vendors or agents? Do they shift the focus to making personal digs, or do they keep it professional? If you ask about a property's vendor, do they tell you insider information, trying to gain trust? Do they speak well or badly?

— Do they have capacity themselves or with their team?

— What other listings do they have coming up?

When an agent is working for you, you want them to be as professional as possible, not compromising your position with a purchaser. I look out for unreturned phone calls, speaking ill or sharing 'secrets' about the vendors they are working for. How do they present? Do you trust them? Do they work hard and well as a team? Will they rise above the pack scuffling and elbowing each other or will they take the time to understand what you are looking for as a purchaser and think about any properties that might suit you, even if you have let them know this one is not quite right?

One of the best agents I have worked with kept a running board in his office that was used to match purchasers who were looking for a property with ones that were coming up or that other agents had seen. The list that I have seen in passing over the years includes the potential purchaser, what type of home they want and a potential price range. They would have more detail on file, but by displaying the potential purchasers and the homes that they have seen, are coming to market or are listed in this way, they can start mentally making connections.

On a number of occasions, this agent has sold my property to one of these purchasers before it has been formally listed and taken to market. They have also introduced the purchaser to a property by twisting their arm to come and check it out when they had lost interest in looking or had checked out of the intense looking process for a while.

This is the power of a team that does the work in the busy and the quiet times.

Before signing up with an agent

There are a couple of other things to keep in mind when you're ready to sign up with an agent.

Agents' fees

Agents' fees will vary from the fixed price percentage. I have seen percentages ranging from 1 to 3 per cent, some with inclusions and many without.

Table 7.2 sets out a state-by-state breakdown according to *realestate.com.au*.

Table 7.2: Average agents' fees across Australia

	Metro	Regional
NSW	1.8–2.5%	2.5–3.5%
Vic.	1.6–2.5%	2.5–3.5%
Qld	2–2.5%	2.5–3.5%
SA	2–2.75%	2.75-3%
WA	2.2%	3%+
Tas. (state average)	3.25%	
ACT	2–2.5%	2.0–2.5%
NT (territory average)	2.8%	

One of the major considerations that determines the range in which your fees will sit is the value of the home you are selling. If you are selling a $3 million home vs a $1 million home, you might expect the fees to be higher on the lower priced listing. If your home has a complex sales strategy — for example, off the plan, or house and land — you can expect a higher commission as there is more work involved.

There is a big difference in the amount of commission to agents, depending on the value of the home. Selling a $3 million home at 2 per cent commission is $60000, whereas its counterpart at $1 million will be $20000. If we took the upper and lower range of the $1 million home, it might cost $16000 to $25000. Some agents may include marketing costs in their commission, but in my experience these are generally extras that get added on top.

The agent's experience and the team around them will also be factored into the commission. I don't usually mind when an agent is willing to fight for or justify their fees because I want them to be able to do this for me when I am on the market.

Another way that agents often sell property is to use a bonus structure or sliding scale. I have seen this work out really well for them in a rising market! Say our $1 million property is listed with a 2 per cent commission up to $1 million, the agent could suggest that they earn a larger percentage for anything above this amount — up to, say, 10 per cent. So, if your property, listed at an upper amount of $1 million, sold for $1.2 million and you agreed to this commission structure, you would be paying:

Property listed price x commission percentage ($1 000 000 x 2 per cent)	$20 000
Amount over listed price x scaled percentage ($20 000 x 10 per cent)	+ $20 000
Total commission	$40 000

The question you need to ask when looking at the structure is, 'Do you think the agent will be working harder or fighting harder to achieve that extra $200 000 if they receive a 10 per cent commission or not?' I am unsure if there is actually a good answer for this. I have seen this work well and not so well. You may also decide to limit or cap the bonus. So you might offer 10 per cent to a cap of $15 000, which would mean you are limiting the commission to $35 000.

Exclusivity period

It is also common for agents to have an exclusivity period during which they are the only agent who is allowed to sell this property. This might be 30, 60, 90 days or longer, depending on the type of property you are selling. The default period in Victoria is 60 days.

Consider the time frame you are agreeing to in light of the expected sales date and how long you will work with an agent after this period. Agents are incentivised to sell. They don't receive any payment unless they make this happen, so it is reasonable that they are given a period of time after the private sale or auction date, but you do want to reconsider if you are unhappy and there is no movement on the property and you might be able to list with another agent.

Style your property for success

Okay, with your agent hired, you're now ready to enter into the final stages of preparing your property for sale, beginning with styling your property. Wow, this space has advanced so much in the past 10 years! Furniture is the jewellery that brings a home to life. This area of the project makes such a difference.

Why is styling important? This all comes back to what you are selling: the dream. You can do all you want with incredible finishes and re-finishing the space, but if you don't tie it all together with the right furniture you will be leaving money on the table. The purpose of the styling is to show the spaces in their best light, bringing an emotional connection and impact to the potential purchaser. This should present a picture to potential purchasers of how they could be living their best life in this home.

The biggest impacts I have seen are when homes have been decluttered and the right-size furniture has been brought in to highlight the space.

You have a decision to make. Will you style it yourself or will you get someone in? Can you get away with the furniture you have if you are living in it? This is the time when you need to think critically: can you do this better? Are your skills up to scratch and do you have enough time to do this work? There is a cost involved in hiring a stylist, obviously, but there are also other implications. For instance, if you live in the house you may need to move out. You might even need to hire a storage unit to move your furniture into. I have seen properties completely transformed by styling to the value of $50 000 or more.

Next, I will discuss some of the implications of styling. There is no right or wrong here. The question is just what can you do and what will give your sale the best impact?

If you live in the house

This is great as you have somewhere to live — but this also means you will be living in the home while the house is on the market.

How fun! My partner and I have done this many times with four kids in tow. It is a lot of cleaning, a lot of hiding things and a little bit of stress to have the perfect home at all times. In honesty, I do enjoy selling houses I am not living in much, much more. The agents often like it more too as they can get access to the house at any time that suits them and the potential purchaser, without having to call the vendor and book in a time. Much more convenient.

In some instances, though, there is a love and warmth that comes from a home that is working, a home that is in action, being used and loved. It feels less staged — who would have thought! — and more real and relatable. However, if you are planning on doing this you need to be living the dream life for a moment.

Pro tips

— *Be critical of your circumstances. Understand your capacity to live through the sales process and evaluate whether or not it will be worth it for you.*

— *Decluttering is your best friend, and when you do it you will wonder why you didn't do it earlier. Move everything out that doesn't have a place — when in doubt, remove it! The one caveat to this is if you have a style that is eclectic, stylish and full — then you may not need to declutter — but in general, less is more!*

— *The final stage of getting ready for sale is really about being clean, clean, clean! This is in every area of your home. In the fridge — um, yes, your fridge should read like a mean, green, colour-coordinated veggie monster. What about your drawers? Do they need to be perfect? Yes, of course they do. People snoop, and remember that this house is the magic ingredient they need to have a perfect life. Your drawers demonstrate this with their perfect organisation and order.*

I know my version of how you get ready to go to market is a little extra, but it really helps set the scene. All the things I can control are controlled.

Hiring a stylist

Most people will actually need to hire a stylist to get ready for market, particularly if they are not living in the home. Furnishing a house is a lot of work and requires quite a lot of furniture — the bedrooms alone in a four-bedroom house would need:

— four king, queen or double beds

— four sets of linen, cushions, etc.

— eight bedside tables

— eight lamps

— side chairs

— artwork.

You might not have this amount of spare furniture, particularly when you start out. If this is the case, it may be worth hiring a stylist to furnish the house.

I recommend getting quotes from several companies as they will vary in price, but also in style. Generally, you will not get to select how they style your home, but you can get an indication of the type of furniture they have in stock and how they furnish a home by the work they have done previously.

You will want to get a quote for them to furnish the home for the sales period, but you will also need to know what the weekly rental rate would be — in case you need to keep the home furnished after the closing date of the sale.

Styling the home yourself

The alternative to this would be furnishing the home yourself. Let's say a styling company charges $10 000 to style your home, then perhaps for each build you have a $10 000 budget. This is what I prefer to do. I love nice furniture and being able to purchase a few things at the end of a build. I will rarely purchase anything for our home if I don't have a house sale coming up. Giving myself the styling budget to update some pieces in our home has allowed us to grow our collection. Though, apparently my photographer is getting a little bored of seeing the same things in my homes!

I am always on the lookout on Facebook marketplace for artworks and eclectic styling pieces that will photograph well.

 Pro tips

My top tips for styling a home on a budget include:

— *Use second-hand beds from marketplace; you will not be sleeping in them so that's not a concern.*

— *I have sets of linen I imported that I use for our beds at home.*

— *Artwork is one of the biggest requirements. I buy little pieces and frame them when they catch my eye. I also frame kids' art when it is particularly good in colour and it's hard to tell it was done by kids. I buy items that I can then use as birthday gifts, shop at affordable art fairs, cut out pictures in books and frame them, buy items at fundraisers and make things with the kids from old test paint pots. You don't want to be making art in the lead-up to a photoshoot — instead do this early when you have more time.*

I have a collection of coffee-table books that are great to style with and which I have collected over time.

Jars with grains in them are great in pantries.

Ceramics and interesting pieces can be purchased from op shops and marketplace for low prices too. It is always nice to have a different approach to your styling.

Borrow from friends: my house has been packed up countless times and lent out to friends — so much so that it really does give my partner John the irrits! If you have great family or friends who wouldn't mind lending you a thing or two I recommend you jump aboard that train.

I feel like the worst thing you can do when styling a home is have everything feel like it is straight from a retail catalogue or that you have just headed down to Kmart and purchased one of everything. Layering and mixing old and new pieces has worked much better for me, but as I do need the pieces to be pristine, often the ones I live with day to day have had too much use to be shown in a shiny new home.

To prepare for this aspect of the project I work through the build plan with an idea of what I will use in each space. This allows me to create a simple Canva or PowerPoint slide show, which means I can fill out and work out where I am going with the styling along the way.

Remember, the point of renovating for profit is to make a profit. You will really want to think about what you need to spend money on and what you don't. Furnishing bedside table lamps may mean you don't need to buy them.

Final check — we all have that friend who is a little more stylish than us, who knows how to pull it together, or who has a catalogue of things in their brain that you can tap into when you're in a hurry. Call on them to help you in this process. Do your best to set it up, but allow a little time to have them do a final once-over. It's funny how fresh eyes can give a tiny final tweak, which can elevate your space to the next level.

Market your recently completed project

Once you have completed your project, surely your job is done, isn't it? The agent you have hired will take over and make all of the magic happen, won't they? Aren't they going to be the ones organising the photos and floorplans — and everything else? In my experience over the years and with DevelopHers I have seen this done really well, and also really, really poorly.

Perhaps I am too controlling or perhaps I am just looking to take advantage of every extra edge I can get, but I like to work with the real estate agents to control this part of the project. I have at this point spent months working on the project agonising about every detail included in the build, so I want to know that my sales campaign is working to the best of its ability and this, in my view, comes with vendor and agent collaboration.

Researching

Before you begin, let's get your eye tuned in to the local market and what is working in your area.

1. *Have a look at the current listings.*

   - What stands out to you?

   - Why? Is it a punchy image or the style of the house?

   - What do you want to see? Is it the size of the land? A hero shot?

   - Where can your project stand out against the others? How does it fare?

   - What style of photography have they used. Do the homes look warm and welcoming? Are you drawn to go check them out or are you just clicking through without anything catching your attention?

2. *Ask the agents which projects were marketed well.*

   - What did they do well and what was the result?

   - What listings had a heap of traction online?

   - Have a look at the listing and determine whether there is anything you can learn from this.

3. *Look a little further afield.*

   - Are there any projects or houses that have grabbed your attention?

   - Have you seen any listings anywhere else and have you been drawn back to them?

- Articles, agents, social media? Noticing what other people have done well and what you think you might be able to improve on will go a long way.

Organising your marketing

Ultimately, this is all about telling a story and curating the story that you want to tell with the marketing and materials. Your purchaser will be out there, but at any one time not everyone who would like to upgrade their home or who would love your home will be in the market looking. You might have had this experience when you were looking to purchase a project or another home. You jump in and out of the market at different times depending on the priority in among the other priorities in your life and how energised or disheartened you felt by the opportunities that were on the market at any one time.

Think about each piece of your marketing and how it would speak to your potential purchaser. What are they looking for and how will the product you have created fit this brief?

Photos

The photos are all about getting people to your open homes. You want to think critically about how you can use your images to do this. Here are some of the things I consider when thinking about my photos.

The hero shot

I generally have an idea of the best angle or the hero shot that I want to create as I'm building. I am planning this shot and budgeting around making this a really *wow* moment. As a general rule, I tend to find the following images can work particularly well:

— Front façade of a home, particularly if it is heritage

— Kitchen square on to an island bench

— Lounge/dining/living — this can be harder to achieve, but what I look for is an idea of size and space

— Rear garden/façade photograph.

The hero shot is the image that will stand for my home. It is the one that will get the most traction and the one that I rely upon to stop people scrolling on the real estate sites and to get them to take a closer look.

Remember, while you want to show beautiful, architectural images of front-on shots, and close-ups of soft furnishings, don't forget to also show the 'real-estate angle pics'. These will make your space feel spacious and will often show 'more' in each image.

Why is this important? On a recent campaign — a beautiful home that one of our DevelopHers ran — there was no natural hero shot. The images were all beautiful — they looked lovely and well composed — but overall it was hard to get a sense of *wow* from this home. The home looked small when it actually wasn't. Why did this happen? The angles you can get with a camera sometimes don't play in your favour. There was a wall near the kitchen island so a square or front-on image couldn't be taken. The lounge and dining were open plan, but it wasn't possible to capture this in one clean image as, again, the wall and shape of the room prevented this.

What was the solution? After the photographer took images in an editorial style and the first open was completed, the issue was apparent: there weren't enough people coming through the home and a critical look at how it was being marketed revealed this issue. A new image, external this time, was taken and used to show the size of the extension and home, along with a series of more traditional fish-eye images, to demonstrate more of the room sizes and space in the home, and a lesson in hero images and balancing between editorial and traditional real-estate images was learned.

Photograph styles

Traditional real estate photography tends to be captured with fish eye lenses and can be dominated by ceilings and a sea of downlights. This is not my preferred style of images, because while it does show the spaces well, it often lacks an emotional draw — and by now you probably know how I feel about creating an emotional connection.

You will see magazine-style or editorial-style photography in any house-and-garden magazine and if you pick up a few of them you will quickly see that they all have a slightly different style to them.

I like to shoot our homes in an editorial manner as it speaks to the project being a dream home, one that has an emotive draw of the amazing life you will be able to create in this space. These types of images often leave a little of the room uncaptured and to the imagination. I think this also gives the person looking for their dream home a reason to come to the inspection and discover more for themselves. In my opinion, it also points to care of detail and therefore the value of the house you have created, and can help in some markets to differentiate your home from another. I know that some agents can give you push-back on including this type of photography. My preference is to make sure these emotive images are included but to balance these with stylised images that have a wider angle to make sure I am showing both the moments and the space. Please know that you can stand for how you market your home. It is your home to sell and while this may not be common practice it is infiltrating online marketing.

Choosing a photographer

Agents usually have a photographer they deal with all the time. Have a look at their work and think about whether this will be right for you and your project instead of blindly trusting this will bring the best outcome.

In our community, many of the women have found that selecting different photographers from the one recommended by the agent has met with significant push-back. You need to do what is right for you and explain this to the agent. Understand what images they need, and try to provide that within your brief.

I generally use my own photographer — a quick look at any of my homes will show you who I like to use — for a few reasons:

— We work incredibly well together and there is a built-up understanding of how we can best highlight features.

— The images I have of a home are my one-offs to show the finished product of the home that I have spent countless hours working on — I really want to capture as much of this as I can.

— I will often take up to 60 images in a home and I will use them for branding and the website, to highlight key suppliers and help build relationships.

Pro tip

Gift some images that highlight your suppliers' work to them (if your photographer will allow it). Suppliers often get involved in one aspect of a build — say windows — and then never see the finished and styled project. I love keeping a list of suppliers and sending out the images to all who were involved for them to use on their socials as an additional note of appreciation. Hopefully, the carpenters and trades are proud of their work on the project and understand how much we appreciate them. I love it when they bring their family through opens to show them the work they have been doing.

Dusk or daytime images?

For me there are no hard and fast rules here — the house needs to be captured when it is looking its best. I have had contemporary homes (probably most) that really look best in daylight. However, homes like my James St home really looked best at dusk when the warm glow of lighting highlighted the mid-century feel. Sometimes, I will make sure I get a selection of both so I can work with whatever suits the particular use of the image.

Listing online

In my market there are two major players in this space, Domain and REA. I list on both but I also know that our markets have a strong preference for one over the other. I will leave it up to you, but if you are selling in a public manner these are really the best places you can get the word out there.

These sites already have a listing for your home address and other sites scrape this data and share it. The world of having all the information is here so you can generally see most, if not all, of the transactions on a property and the images used to list it. It is such an invaluable tool for people buying and selling.

The sites will display one 'hero' image on the search and then other images as the viewer clicks through. I do not upload all my images, but I also upload more than would be typical. I select the order of these images so that I take the viewer on a journey through the home — so it feels intentional and thought-out and doesn't present as a jumble of images. I have the façade as the hero or second image, followed by walking through the home into key areas such as the kitchen and lounge/dining areas before moving to bedrooms.

I want people to get a sense of the home early online and even if the bedrooms are the front of the home, they are secondary spaces so they appear later.

Floorplans

I always do floorplans in a stylised way for my projects. This really helps people who are considering the home to understand whether it could be the best fit for them and it is the best way for people to see whether they need to make the effort to inspect a home.

In our inner-city markets it would be a rare home that didn't offer this piece of information with the property for sale, and the cost to complete this work is relatively low cost.

Copywriting

Many of the inner-city agencies have skilled copywriters who will view your home and put together all the bits of copy you will need for the various listings. Sometimes the agent will do this.

For me, it forms part of the story, so I always personally review and consider what has been submitted, sometimes re-writing pieces of information.

Marketing boards

Physical marketing boards on the property are a massive driver of traffic in an online world! How often have you driven past a property and stopped to look at the board? I know, right? We all love a sticky beak.

I add a small 'coming soon' line at the bottom of the board to get people to watch the project's progress, but I will only do this once the façade is near completion — the garden and painting might not be finished, but I'm getting close to the finish line and the house is looking good.

I then move to a more significant marketing board with images of the home. This is where I look again to how I'm displaying it. If my board has three landscape images on it — a bigger one on top and then two smaller ones under it (this is one of the standard configurations) — I will make sure I have a landscape hero image — not of the façade because they are standing in front of this — and a bathroom and kitchen to draw people into the home. Bedrooms often just show the bed and some styling so unless there is a real drive to this it becomes secondary.

Brochures

I love having brochures for my homes. These always have a selection of images and the floorplan on them, although I have used many formats over the years. These are a great investment, in my eyes, as they are something for a potential purchaser to take with them and mull over while they are having a coffee or discussing the home with their partner. It triggers the memory and doesn't hide the home in an online space that you need to look up.

There are many formats, and often the agent will have their own format that they use for ease and simplicity. All the marketing pieces need to coordinate quickly once you have the images, floorplan and copy.

Print publications

Sometimes you might be offered print publication options. I tend not to use these unless there is a specific market that they will target. You do need to work out whether this is an expense that makes sense for your project.

One of the incredible agents I have worked with, and discussed this with at great length, argues that it is a touch point for the handful of purchasers that are interested in the home — a point where they can see the value and exclusiveness of the property.

Letterbox drops

Letterbox drops are sometimes proposed by agents. This is where you drop a DL flyer of your property into the letterboxes of your neighbouring streets and suburbs using an 'on the market' or a 'coming soon' strategy.

This is not something I would usually invest in, but I have received a number of these flyers over the years. I feel like it is marketing the agent and agency that has listed the property for you more than the house. A recent drop that I did to 1000 homes had only one enquiry generated from it and you would be targeting a very passive market that is not really looking. The effectiveness of letterbox drops is volume. If you are going to invest in this strategy, you need to do a large number — that is, 10 000 plus for urban listings.

Online advertorials

This is where you might do a paid feature with an online site to reach a larger audience — think The Design Files for a designer home that is Melbourne based, or some mid-century homes might benefit from being listed on a specific Instagram or influencer site that people are following for this specific content.

I have seen this strategy work really well to get many people to an interesting home or to widen the audience beyond the area and suburb. Weigh up the potential to find your purchaser in this way, and also the cost. Depending on the publication and market, this can be a great way to prove to your purchasers that this home is special as it has been featured. Peer acceptance can also drive a sense of FOMO and I love this for my homes.

Video content

Agents are pushing this more and more for property video content. There is a value here, if it can be used across different platforms such as REA, social media and real estate agency websites. I feel like it is only for a particular market and as with all types of marketing you need to weigh up your return on investment before you sign off on spending more. I used video in a few of my campaigns — most notable was the James Street one, which, due to the way it was shot by Flip Films, added to the mid-century vibes and set the scene of an entertainer's home.

Generating hype

With the paid listing sections of marketing your project covered, let's go guerrilla — let's think about what else you can do, now that the intense part of getting your house ready for the market is done.

Open-house events

Have you got a special home that would benefit from an open-house event? I have used these several times for a few of my homes, where I know the home is at its best when it is hosting parties and entertaining. It allows people to hang out for a while and suck in the atmosphere. I wouldn't say it is right for all homes — but for the right one, do it!

Features in publications

How will you help generate publicity for your home? A bit of good PR didn't hurt anyone! If there is a blog or a local paper that this would work wonders for — or if there is an interesting angle that one of the real estate online accounts, or Instagram accounts would be interested in — then by all means send it to them!

But don't be lazy here. Think about the angle that will work for each account — for example, a renovating blog/Insta account might be interested in the transformation and your top tips, whereas a local paper or print magazine might be interested in the human interest side and might want an image of you and your family. If you put a little effort into creating an angle for them and then having a series of images that they can use in the email with a link to the rest, you will have a better chance at getting picked up.

I can tell you that people send in article requests all the time. They are generic and relentless and usually have nothing to do with our audience. I will stop and engage only with ones I can see visually are going to be a good fit and benefit to my audience and also make things easy for me to work with and get going quickly.

Make sure you include a document in the image file that has the following:

— Photographer's details and handles

— Suppliers used if you want them included in tags and articles — for example, Builder: Beirin Projects, @beirinprojects, or Carpet: Jagers Carpets, @jagerscarpets, product: Carrama 54.

Doing things like this limits the back and forth and really helps to streamline the process, ensuring that there is credit for the right people throughout.

Distributing images to suppliers

In the same way as you just sent these images to potential promoters, remember that all of your product suppliers and trades are also potential advocates of your home. I try to make a list of as many people who worked on the project as possible and then look through the images for all the building and furnishing suppliers I can think of and send them a little note.

I like to personalise the note, if I can, with the name of my contact. But if it is a bigger company — for instance, retailer West Elm — I will sometimes also send it to marketing to make sure that it is received at the right place.

I let them know that I enjoyed their product and what it was that I liked about it; that this is my current project and that it is on the market; that I would love them to share it, preferably before the sale date; and then I give them some details that they can use in their post, along with key suppliers that I want included in all posts:

Project by:

Designer:

Builder:

On the market with agent:

Photographer:

I find that this is really well received and can start to create a buzz around a home coming up to the auction day or during the campaign. The algorithms then start working for you as they know if people have engaged with this property they will be shown other similar ones.

And maybe your home will follow your potential purchaser around the internet until they start paying attention!

Preparing for opens

Bake those cookies!

Why do people recommend that you bake cookies right before an open home? Well, it is not just to leave a nice little gift for the real estate agents to eat, but also to demonstrate that the people who live here have a life so wonderful that they have time to bake cookies for their guests that leave the home smelling wonderful. The cookies, especially if I bake them, will not get someone to buy a home, but can entice them to think about how they might cook in this home.

While you might not bake cookies, especially if it is a home you are not living in and you haven't run the oven yet, there are other things you can do:

— Turn on the lights and lamps to give a homely feel.

— Light candles and make sure there is a nice smell in the home.

— Display fresh flowers.

- Hang new, clean towels in the bathroom.

- Set background music.

- Make sure the home is clutter free and styled to show its best light. (This can be eclectic. In my opinion it doesn't need to be without personality — I can find these homes boring.)

- Think about inside those cupboards — you know people open them to see what is inside. If they open cupboards that are overflowing or filled with dirty renovation tools it will leave a sense of query on the size of the space or the attention to detail.

- Make sure the home is warm or cool depending on the weather.

- If it is winter and an open fire is a central feature, be sure to light this.

- Get the garden looking in its best light. This might mean blowing paths daily or raking fallen leaves — don't let them think about the chores that need to be done when they live here.

You want to do this set-up yourself, and you should arrive early to do this. Often on a busy weekend the purchasers will arrive early too. You want the agents to focus on setting themselves up to sell your home, rather than running around doing all the small lighting and music things. Just think of it from their perspective: if an agent is showing six homes on a Saturday and each one needs lights on and off and a different set of actions to get that home ready, it would be so easy to forget to turn on music and they may not have time to have that all-important conversation with the next purchaser of your home.

Keeping up the energy

I always find that the time when your home is on the market is the hardest part of selling.

Why?

Because you can't really control anything. You can send around photos, and you can make the house nice for opens, but the decisions have been made, the process has run its course and now you have a product listed and it is judgement day.

The small comments are hurtful, and ultimately helpful, but this is the time when you start hearing about the flats next door or the size of the block, or whether people do or don't like your selection of stone. Everyone is a critic — but it is someone gutsy, someone really admirable, who will do the work to get a home renovated and ready to be sold.

My advice: focus on what you can control, tweak the listings, listen to the agents, attend other open homes, get the details on the property right...and clean, clean, clean. Then get out of your own head! This could be the time to look at other houses to purchase and to distract yourself with possibilities, but even though you might feel exhausted, go the extra mile to make sure your home is shown in the best light possible.

Make sure you check in at least weekly — do the cleans, set the scene, replace the flowers, promote and advocate for your baby — because, after all, you have put your time and energy into sweating the details to this point. It would be a shame to drop the ball on the home straight!

Here is a learning lesson for you.

I generally feel quite exhausted at the end of a run up to finishing a project. There is always a big push and somehow there always seems to be a sense of 'emergency' to get onto the market: quick, before school holidays; or hurry, before Christmas break.

What this means is that there are many details coming together at the last minute and these things need to be coordinated. I am now getting better at avoiding the rush, but gosh it can be a challenge!

The lead-up to one of my earlier houses was a bit of a challenge. We had guests staying with us from Canada, and we had a few projects on the go and little kids and babies to juggle. I somehow ended up with conjunctivitis from one of the kids so it looked like I was crying all the time, and there was only one day available to style a house from when the internal scaffold came down.

While this epic transformation would have performed really, really well from an online sense, it was a big push and I was tired. As a result, here are the things that were not completed during the campaign:

— There was dust behind the bathroom door (I know this because someone wrote a note about it and then told us. Eek...embarrassing)

— I didn't have the door angle installed to the big sliding doors. I could have caulked this, but instead I like to do metal angles as they last better, covering the gap between the frame and the concrete cut. This meant that there was a gap that was not finished of about 10 mm or less where you walk.

— I put the flowers and plants in at the beginning of the campaign, but didn't replace them regularly enough throughout the campaign.

The result: one potential purchaser brought a builder through who picked the detail of the trims and made the comment, 'If they haven't even finished this, which you can see, imagine what you can't see'. This ended up losing me this keen purchaser and you can't afford to lose purchasers on stupid mistakes, regardless of whether you have a hot market or not.

The campaign went well: there were photos on the cover of *Domain Magazine*, and it had great traction, but when people came to the home, old flowers greeted them — and frankly this told people I didn't care, which could not have been further from the truth — but I didn't have my eye on the prize and my delivery was sloppy.

While I can only tell you I lost one purchaser for sure and I don't know if they would have bid on auction day, I can tell you that I was complacent. I was off the back of a huge auction where there were 500 people in the crowd and I didn't bring the same level of baking cookies and sweating the small details to this home — even though I had spent all my time, energy and cash making it as amazing as it could be and the result was felt in the demand.

I won't make this mistake again.

Q&A on selling properties that have been recently renovated for profit

I thought it would be good to get insights from an expert in the realm of selling properties, so I spoke to my friend Sam. I have been lucky enough to be working with Sam Rigopoulos from Jellis Craig. Sam has been recognised as one of the top agents and is a past recipient of the REIV Sales Person of the Year award. He has been a top agent within the Jellis Craig group, and ranked first in the Real Estate Business Top 50 as well as receiving many other awards.

Alongside his team, Sam consistently delivers outstanding results, with over 170 homes sold each year in inner-city Melbourne. As the leader of the Jellis Craig Inner North group, Sam also oversees the management of 2500 rental properties and the sale of approximately 1000 homes annually across three offices.

One of the things I have loved about working with Sam over the past 10+ years is that he has relentlessly pursued to better the experience for the vendor and purchaser, and his insights into the evolving market — and it has really evolved over this time, combined with his practical, day-to-day approach to running phenomenal property campaigns that offer valuable insight into the industry.

Here are his thoughts and top tips on creating the best possible outcome for your sale.

Things vendors can do to maximise their outcomes

When it comes to maximising your outcome/price from any transaction in property there are a few key pillars to align. Some are easy, some take a little leap of faith, but all are critical.

These pillars are:

— *Presentation*: from the street appeal (first impression) to the reflective moment (in the rear yard looking back

(continued)

at the house) buyers should see the house in the best possible light. The gardens, the painting, the clutter and of course the styling should all be addressed, as should any handyman/trade items around the house. A crisp, clean, well-presented home provides buyers with confidence that it has been well maintained or renovated — peace of mind in this regard is priceless. Add to this aspirational furniture/styling and the stage is set for that dream home feeling.

— *Marketing:* to highlight the home and ensure it is favoured above others it must jump off the screen in a buyer's search. The hero shot should be special and commanding. The quality of photography should be sharp — well produced in post production — and suited to the style of the home. Consider day shoots, dusk shoots, dawn shoots and drone shoots.

What will you do to ensure this home looks special? Add a human element to the images? Throw in some editorial style images? There is always something distinct that can be done for each campaign to separate it from the pack.

Quality videography, social media and an estate agent's data base/network should all combine to leave no stone unturned in reaching the widest audience possible.

Don't spend millions on a renovation and skimp on conduit to your buyers: the marketing!

— *Price:* make sure your price attracts buyers to the home. If a home is overpriced even the greatest marketing production will not overcome this challenge. Every home has a push and pull price. In the first instance pricing of a home should be logical and easily supported by data. If the market is stable and the data is easily supporting the price, the market will be able to logically connect with the home and quickly move past that hurdle and into the emotive state of mentally picturing which kid gets which bedroom (and so on). Once buyers are in this mode you are halfway to sold — a high price keeps them stuck in over-analysis of the logical components and the longer they are there the less likely they are to move to an emotive state. The peak time for a campaign to be well priced to attract interest is in the first 1 to 10 days. This is when the house will be at the height of exposure to the hottest buyers in the market. This is when you need to pull the strongest audience in and connect them emotionally with the home.

Working with a real estate agent

You should start working with an agent as early as possible in the process. This allows the agent/agency to track key buyer leads during your build/renovation, which can provide invaluable feedback on the pending campaign as well as an opportunity to connect dots between house and buyers off market if possible.

That said, the most impactful aspect of early engagement is advice on what to include in your project, how to cater for the buyers who are most likely to drive an outcome and advice on how you can reverse engineer your design and layout to suit the needs of the strongest possible buyers for the product type you are creating.

Selecting and engaging the right real estate agent

My top tips for selecting an agent are:

— Ensure they have a strong track record of dealing with campaigns in your intended price range and/or suburb. A sustained and successful track record doesn't happen by accident. It means that agent or agency have a habit of creating successful outcomes. They are meeting the right buyers and can create the right outcomes.

— Check that there is a quality team to support the lead agent. A quality team can resource themselves to deep dive through data, refer buyers and manage appointments so as not to miss opportunities. The very

(continued)

best agents have a support network of some description — it is critical to a campaign's performance.

— Watch how they treat people at open for inspections, and assess their track record of sales or clearance rates. Does this reflect well?

Never select an agent on fee. Anyone who is willing to compromise their own pay to gain business will most likely act similarly when negotiating with a buyer to conclude a deal. The way they do one thing is typically the way they do everything. Understand what is a fair fee for the market and reward the agent well to get the best results.

Sales campaign type and method

Each home is different, but essentially if the house looks good, feels good and is well marketed the strategy of the campaign can be auction, private sale or EOI. Your agent should recommended a method that suits the property type and the buyer pool for your area.

Unless you have a particularly strong preference, the best thing to do is allow the agent space to guide you. Look at past successes and failures within your market to understand the result and use them as case studies giving context to the current conditions of the day to make an informed decision on your strategy.

A quick recap

— The first 10 to 14 days of a sales campaign are the most critical for buyer interest. Keep up your energy so you can plan and execute this final aspect of the build to perfection.

— Preparing your property for sale is key. It involves finishing renovations and assembling the right team — from agents to stylists and conveyancers — and planning every detail of the sales process.

— From high-impact photography to strategic copywriting, when marketing your property ensure it tells a compelling story. Hero shots, professional floorplans and detailed brochures can significantly boost buyer interest.

— Styling your property elevates its appeal by showcasing it as a dream home. Focus on creating an emotional connection for buyers. Make sure your home is clutter free and stands out in your market.

— Be market savvy: understand the market conditions and analyse your competition. This involves strategic pricing, choosing the right sales method and maintaining flexibility to adjust based on market feedback.

— Whether you opt for an auction, private sale or expression of interest, your choice should align with your property's unique strengths and the current market dynamics. Work with your team, particularly your agent, to make key decisions about the sales method.

— Make sure you engage an agent you can trust who aligns with your vision, communicates well and can negotiate effectively on your behalf.

— Selling, like all the other aspects of renovating for profit, is a process of refinement. Learn from each campaign to improve future projects, focusing on small details that leave lasting impressions on buyers.

Putting it all together

Congratulations! You now have all the tools you need to play the renovation game. We have covered:

— 'why you' and building courage

— how to unlock feasibilities so you know what a profitable renovation looks like

— creating a unique value proposition that fits with your vision and where you are at

— financing and funding

— buying the right property

— managing the project

— selling successfully.

All you need to do is pull it all together — to move your gears into action and start playing this game! Before you do, however, I thought it would be prudent to look at some things to dodge.

Seven cash-sucking money pits to avoid!

In the world of property development and renovation, it's all too easy to fall into financial traps that can drain your resources and derail your projects. Here are seven common money pits to steer clear of, along with practical advice on how to avoid them.

1. Inaction has a cost!

We're all busy, but when you're running a project, you set the pace. Inaction and procrastination can be incredibly costly.

— *Make decisions quickly and effectively.* The ability to make swift and informed decisions is crucial. Delaying decisions can result in increased holding costs and disrupt the project's flow.

— *Determine what information you need.* Identify the key information required to make decisions and actively seek it out. Don't let unknowns stall your progress.

— *Avoid long deliberations.* Prolonged deliberations can significantly impact your project timeline and budget. Set deadlines for decision making to maintain momentum.

Pro tip

Use a decision matrix to evaluate options quickly and move forward without unnecessary delays.

2. Planning risks and controllable actions

Understanding the planning costs and potential risks associated with your project site is essential.

— *Know your planning costs.* Investigate the costs associated with obtaining the necessary approvals and permits for your site. This includes consulting fees and potential modifications.

- *Assess the feasibility of your plans.* Ensure that your intended plans for the site are viable. Will the planning process be straightforward or fraught with challenges?

- *Calculate site compromises.* Assess whether compromises on the site could negatively impact your return on investment (ROI). Know when the costs outweigh the benefits.

- *Identify easy vs hard paths.* Recognise when there's an easy route and a difficult one. Understanding the costs associated with each can help you make informed decisions.

Pro tip

Consult with a town planner early in the process to get a clear understanding of potential hurdles and associated costs.

---

3. Contingency and project accuracy

Overly optimistic feasibilities that don't account for the realities of your vision can lead to financial pitfalls.

- *Ensure feasibilities are accurate.* Spend the necessary time to create accurate feasibility studies. This reduces your reliance on contingencies and market growth to cover unexpected expenses.

- *Use contingencies wisely.* The goal of a contingency fund is to remain untouched. It should be a safety net, not a crutch.

Pro tip

Include a buffer in your budget for unforeseen expenses, but strive to keep within the initial feasibility.

---

4. Material and product selection and how this relates to your ROI

Material and product creep is a common issue that can drain your budget without adding value.

— *Avoid material creep.* It's easy to be enticed by the latest and greatest products. However, not all upgrades will provide a significant ROI (return on investment).

— *Assess ROI on selections.* Before opting for high-end finishes, consider whether they will truly add value to your property. Some investments may appeal more to personal tastes than to potential buyers.

Pro tip

Stick to what the market expects for your type of property and location. Sometimes, simpler choices yield better financial outcomes.

---

5. Market forces and opportunity costs

The opportunity cost of having your capital tied up in a prolonged project can be significant.

— *Understand opportunity cost.* If your money is stuck in a project for longer than necessary, it might be better utilised elsewhere. Delays can mean missed opportunities in a dynamic market.

— *Market changes.* Beware of how market fluctuations can impact your project. Sometimes, cutting your losses and reallocating resources can be the best strategy.

Pro tip

Regularly review your project timeline and financial commitments to ensure your capital is being used efficiently.

6. The time you sit out inactively is costing you!

Continual action and learning are crucial to making consistent progress.

— *Keep moving forward.* Successful developers rarely strike gold with just one or two projects. Instead, they continually learn, adapt and keep playing the game.

— *Adapt and learn.* Each project is a learning opportunity. Use what you learn to improve your next project and avoid previous mistakes.

Pro tip

Set short-term goals and milestones to maintain momentum and keep your projects moving forward.

7. The right advice from the right people

Doing your own due diligence is essential, as not all advice is created equal.

— *Be selective with advice.* Everyone has opinions on real estate, but not all opinions are valuable. Be selective about who you listen to and validate the information you receive.

— *Recognise motivations.* Understand the underlying motivations of those giving advice. For example, a real estate agent's primary goal is to sell a property, which might not always align with your best interests.

Pro tip

Cross check advice with multiple sources and rely on trusted experts in the field.

These are some of the ways I have seen money siphoned out of projects. All are avoidable with the right approach and mindset.

Case study: Creative ways to get started without saving a deposit

Project overview

Agreed Value	$3 050 000
Price Sold	$3 420 000
Renovation	$92 500
Time	Eight weeks in 2024

Kristen's story of partnering with a property owner to undertake a renovation for profit is a perfect example how you can get going on a project with a smaller amount of funds. This project was completed without paying a 20 per cent deposit, stamp duty, the cash to renovate and hold the property. While these deals take more work, patience and persistence to get off the ground they can circumvent the time spent saving to be able to get going.

The project involved revamping spaces and adding those must-have features that would catch buyers' eyes. Even though the journey was full of unexpected challenges — from quirky repairs to frustrating supply delays — the hard work and patience paid off in the end. The upgrades boosted the home's value by a whopping $370 000, and it sold faster than expected!

Kristen is a great example of how the process can run from trusting gut instincts and planning ahead through to how solid research can make all the difference. Kristen shows that even when things feel uncertain, real progress is possible with the right mindset.

Since moving to Australia in 2020 and bringing a real estate background from the United States, DevelopHer Kristen observed how tricky the real estate market can be, and that many sellers are typically not maximising the value of their property. As the founder of Wealth House, she helps to guide sellers through the process and eliminate any barriers keeping sellers from renovating their home. In her latest project, she worked with three siblings who needed help selling their inherited family home in Sandringham, New South Wales.

At a high level what did you do and what were the results?

Worked with three siblings selling an inherited property to make the home more appealing to buyers (there were lots of quirky features and repairs!) and add value. We re-did a bathroom, reconfigured a space to add a study and 5th bedroom, and added some key features buyers in the area look for. We ended up adding $370 000 in value to the home and selling quicker than the market average.

How did you structure your deal?

The siblings had the funds to renovate and were looking mostly for guidance and someone to be on-site. Since it was low risk for me (just my time), it made more sense to offer a fee or a smaller profit share. They decided to go with the fee for more certainty so I got paid as we went along.

(continued)

What value did you see in the project?

It was a large two-storey family home that had lots of space that wasn't being utilised well. It needed to be reconfigured and some key features added to suit what local buyers are looking for, like a dedicated study and walk-in pantry. While it felt like a big transformation in a big house, it was actually a lot of little things together and the total renovation cost was less than $100 000.

How do you look to work with clients at Wealth House?

I'm open to any project where we can see value. Maybe that means a small cosmetic renovation or something more extensive like an addition or knock down re-build. It's really client driven and based on what their needs and goals are. Above that, personality fit is huge. The client needs to be able to trust me and let me drive the project.

What were your biggest learnings on the project?

Order everything earlier than you think you need to. Even if suppliers give you an estimated time frame, double or triple that! We had a few hold ups on things that took much longer to make and deliver than estimated.

Do your own research. Three real estate agents valued the pre-renovated property and priced it much higher than it should have. When I ran the comps, the house was considerably lower. My client was very logical and we walked through the comps so she could clearly see their appraisals were inflated to get the listing. We settled on $3.05 million but after the sales campaign, I think even that number was high. However, it's really about the final sales price and if I was doing a profit share, I would have been happy with the results.

Trust your gut. On the opposite side, when we went to list, the agent downplayed the price and even lowered the price guide to the $2s in the final week. Bidding started at $2.4 million so it was very stressful! Thankfully it ended up exactly in the range I predicted from the very beginning. I've been keeping my eye on the market and nothing had changed so I had to keep reminding myself that we would still likely get there.

Why do you love renovating so much and what is your end game/plan?

I love being able to help people and make a big impact to their lives. This really would have been a hard sale, likely taking months on the market. Not only did I make this process easier for busy siblings, but they're able to walk away with quite a bit of inheritance to buy a first property or make updates to their current home.

My game plan is to continue working with sellers. I'd like to eventually build out a team as this is a service a lot of sellers could use.

Mitigating your optimism or pessimism

We all sit on the continuum of optimistic or pessimistic. This affects how we view property and our outlook for a project. I really like to delve into this as we can get in our own heads and sabotage ourselves before we begin.

I sit on the optimistic bandwagon, particularly when it comes to time. Is this bad? No, it is neither good nor bad: it is fact. It is what I do with that fact that is important. If I don't identify it as one of my quirks (we all have quirks) then I can get to the place of being overwhelmed very easily if I have too many things on the go at one time.

In some ways this helped me to get started. My partner, John, and I are optimistic: we love doing things and as a result we jumped in with enthusiasm and optimism that others lacked. It was a superpower. However, with six kiddos to consider we needed to become more balanced, which is where some of the rules such as 'only take on projects within 5 minutes from home' came from along with other ones that protect us, such as 'we only do our own projects'.

So, where do you sit and what does this mean for you?

Self-assessment of your framework

Ultimately, you will know what your strengths and weaknesses are, no matter how you frame them. They could be keeping you safe or not. This is not about judging you; this is about you recognising where you are at so you can put more balance into your outlook and the numbers you are running. Ask yourself:

— Are you optimistic or pessimistic and in which areas?

— How do you look at things in these areas and how does this affect your judgement?

— How has this worked or not worked for you in the past?

— What can you learn from reviewing the actions you have taken?

Balancing your framing

The reality is that even though we run numbers on a property and it feels like this should be impartial, our framing of how we read the market in a given area and how optimistic or pessimistic we are will play out in these numbers. We have just identified how this is working or not working for us and have noticed the effect this has had on our decisions. Now we need to think about how we balance the books as such and bring this into the foreground while we are looking at property.

- How do you need to balance your framing?

- Have you got a tendency to sit optimistically or pessimistically and how does this play out when you are looking at numbers?

- What can you keep in mind or set up to balance your framing?

For example, knowing that we see opportunity everywhere, we have learned to keep the blinkers on and not to look at opportunities on the market while we are committed — they are distracting and the issue is time, not creativity — and this is an issue that is hard to fix if we want to grow and take on more projects. When we are looking, we know that a project will take longer than we want it to (or that it used to before we had so many other commitments) so then we take this into consideration while we are talking about time frames.

How knowledgeable are you and what are your weaknesses?

Lack of confidence, in my experience, comes from not having done the work — from not understanding all of the outcomes and possibilities. This can make you nervous when looking at things because you don't know what you don't know.

I recently had to buy ponies and a horse for my children — three of them — because to join pony club you have to have your own horse! Talk about jumping in the deep end. I didn't grow up with horses or ponies and as a result of my lack of knowledge I had put off getting one for a year because I didn't have the experience to make good decisions and I didn't invest the time to learn.

I didn't know where to look for a horse, how much I needed to pay, what type of horse was good or bad, or even how to work this out. Additionally, as I am not an experienced rider and have never owned a horse, it was also hard for me to test ride them to make sure they were sound for my children. Buying a pony doesn't seem like that big of a decision, but the more I learned, the harder it was because the wrong decision could be really, really dangerous for our kids. Which I learned when Emily (my 11-year-old) test rode the wrong horse and broke her shoulder — and the more I think about it the luckier I feel that this was the only injury.

So, what did I do to make sure I built up the knowledge?

I surrounded myself with people who knew what they were looking at and for. Each of them has different experiences and backgrounds, but each was really knowledgeable and I trust each of them implicitly.

As I had three guides I could get three perspectives of how they would look to buy a horse and I combined their thoughts and experiences to form my own opinions.

I needed to work out what budget I was comfortable with spending on each one, but I couldn't work this out without understanding what I would be getting at each of the different price points. This meant looking at horses (and trialling a few) at these levels to understand what is creating and diminishing values.

I needed to also set myself up right so that, when I got to the point of having a horse I did want to purchase, I had the facility in place and I could proceed. In this case, paddocks and equipment.

I needed to engage my team of consultants to care for me in this process — not accountants, brokers, agents or builders, but farriers, vets and transporters.

I needed to learn about the characteristics and differences in the products I would be purchasing to work with — not the style of home and construction methods, like you will be looking at, but types of horses (thoroughbreds, quarter horses, Welsh ponies) — and find the style I liked and that would suit us, regardless of other people's opinions.

I also needed to learn a whole new language, which you will too. (OTT (off the track) is now a hard no for me.) Sensitive to leg, hard mouth, head shy, paddock sour, founder, understand the sizing and what that means, and much more. But importantly, in this new language I needed to understand how to read between the lines of the information provided to get the actual information I needed, as well as any red flags.

And even with all of this there was no amount of learning that could beat being on the ground, seeing them in person and jumping on a horse. But the list of things I didn't know and understand from the beginning was huge!

Identify your knowledge gaps

What information do you need and what are your blind spots in building and renovating for profit? How can you fill in the blanks quickly and make sure you build your confidence?

Set a timer for 2 minutes and write a list of all your knowledge gaps. Go fast and, for now, don't worry about how you will get the knowledge or if you need it. Just let your brain run wild and see how many gaps in knowledge you can write down. This game is always changing so I too can write down a tonne as well that I could delve into to better my craft.

Once you have stopped writing, get up, walk around, move a little and come back to your list after a movement break.

Re-write all of your knowledge gaps in an order that makes sense, using one line per item and grouping them into areas that are similar as you go.

Make an action plan to de-risk your knowledge gaps

It's easy to say, but harder to implement in reality. It will take time and effort to really get across each of the areas, but please understand that your knowledge across the board will determine your outcome. When they are grouped, it will be easier to work through them — like things you need to understand from a building standpoint or what is the resale value of a three- vs four-bedroom home in the suburb where you are looking.

Some of these will need a quick google. Others will take a bit of effort and an action plan to get across, while there are others that will be inconsequential, but will just highlight fears that you have about jumping into a new game.

Here is an example of how you might identify a knowledge gap and then simply plan the steps to create the solution.

Knowledge gap: I don't know how much finance I have access to.

Steps to the solution:

1. Complete my tax return.
2. Book a meeting with a mortgage broker.
3. Create a summary of my assets and liabilities.
4. Ask the broker for advice on how to increase my access to funds.
5. Follow up on the conversation about the potential project type to see if it fits.

Just writing the list didn't really help you though, did it? What you actually need to do is to set timelines on each of the items that are causing road blocks (the big blocks that really do stop you from doing anything) so you can start to move through them. So, at this point, go back to that list and set some timelines for completing these tasks. Here is the example from above with timelines.

Knowledge gap: I don't know how much finance I have access to.

Steps to the solution:

1. Complete my tax return by the end of next week.
2. Book a meeting with a mortgage broker tomorrow.
3. Create a summary of my assets and liabilities and gather the information I think a broker will need.
4. Ask the broker for advice on how to increase my access to funds and run scenarios at the meeting.
5. Follow up on the conversation about the potential project type to see if it fits one week after the meeting.

I have found that sometimes the enormity of the information you need to swallow can make it hard for some people to jump in (generally more pessimistic or anxious people). Others (possibly more optimistic people) just jump in and paddle at break-neck speed to overcome the things that they overlooked. As with everything, the beauty is in the balance: learning what you can and overcoming issues as they come up.

Big things often have small beginnings

You are here for a reason, and frankly, my guess is you wouldn't have read this far into the book if you weren't really wanting to get stuck into this game.

But what do you do if you're starting with a small amount of funds or limited serviceability?

Here's the thing: it doesn't matter if you have a lot or a little at this stage of your journey; it is more about the effort and your progress moving forward. It can be scary to start with because it can be hard to commit to doing something new and unknown. It is rarely worth taking the easy path. It is the challenges — the way we challenge what we are told we should be doing to choose our own adventures — that will make us stronger and help us reap the rewards.

So, as not many of us don't start with massive amounts of money, we need to think about ways we can leverage our time, effort and the funds we actually have available. I admit that things are simpler if you do have money and leverage from the outset because you can just go and purchase a property, complete the renovations and put it back on the market without thinking about how you will fund each aspect. While this process (the one I have spoken about throughout the book) is going to take some effort and understanding, it is relatively simple. It is a bit less simple and more involved if you don't have the funds to just go and do what you want where you want to.

So then, if you don't have money, can you still play the game? Yes, yes, yes — of course you can, but it will require a little extra effort and creativity (possibly like the extra effort that was required to save money or to build the wealth that would allow the people that have more cash to move forward).

Here are some options you could potentially look at.

Seller joint ventures / pre-sale renovations

This is where you complete renovations on a property before it goes to market with the understanding that the renovations will increase the value of the property. The deal can be structured in various ways as you can see in the case study about Kristen who set up a business doing pre-sale renovations for clients; or in the story about Rebecca, who has worked on seller joint ventures (JVs) where she is renovating houses owned by someone else and splitting the income.

Joint ventures (JVs)

Chapter 4 covers the facts on JVs and examples. I have witnessed many examples of DevelopHers JVs working and coming together to create great projects in Queensland, Victoria, New South Wales, Western Australia and the ACT. It is great to see these DevelopHers working together as part of a community and I get to see their successes as well.

Every JV structure on these projects is different. It is important to set one up that is right for you. I have seen many types of JV agreements, including examples of no-cash contributions and ones where everyone makes equal cash and management contributions. One story I love is of Laura, who pitched, set up and ran her first JV with no experience and no money and now runs a huge property business working in this space. She didn't have the money to invest in a project, but she invested time into learning the process, and building relationships with real estate agents and investors alike, so that when she found the right opportunity she was able to act on it and this launched a new pathway for her future.

Redrawing equity or selling an asset

I mention this one because it's often not considered, mainly because the idea of selling, say, your family home, doesn't appeal. The thing is, people are sometimes not aware of the possibilities this can offer — or perhaps they don't want to sell their family home to get started in this space because it feels like they are going backwards.

While I am not suggesting that you should sell your home or re-draw equity from it, I do know it was necessary for us to sell our family home before we could move forward in this space — we would not have been able to start without taking this leap.

I do a lot of consults with DevelopHers who want to learn and invest, and I often see that they haven't understood how to leverage the equity in their homes to be able to play the game. This has left them feeling stuck, but once we are able to unlock this piece of the puzzle the options are much more plentiful.

Accessing development finance

Development finance (which I detailed in chapter 4) is a specific type of finance that is used for developments. It has a higher interest rate and different terms, but looks at different variables. It takes into account the end value of your development or product rather than your income because the assumption is that you will be selling the asset to pay down any debts.

When servicing has been an issue but the project stacks up and there is a really clear pathway to realise the profits, then development finance can be an excellent option for this type of project. It can be a solution for someone who needs a large wage (which often leads to a lack of time and capacity in mental load) to be able to play the game. We used development finance on projects such as Rathmines Street, Clarke Street and Latham Street as we have found them really helpful for JV projects.

There are other options that can be considered, but these are specific and require particular circumstances or situations, so they are a great tool to have in your toolbox but not necessarily applicable to all projects.

Vendor finance

This is where a seller of a property might finance the purchase of that property at a certain interest rate for a specific time. This might be an option if you are purchasing a property where the vendor does not require the funds immediately or it is a buyer's market and the vendor really needs to exit.

Options deals

With an option deal, you purchase the option to buy a property at a time in the future after you have changed the use of that property.

For example, you purchase an option on a block of land, then change the use to 12 townhouses via development approval or a planning permit, and once approved, you purchase the property — but you are not required to go ahead with the purchase if the permit is not realised. You are also able to sell the option to another party not settling the property.

Using a SMSF to develop a property or invest in a JV

This would require you to speak to a financial adviser about your situation, but I have seen this successfully done by DevelopHers in our community and I have also purchased property with a SMSF (self-managed super fund). The advantages are that the banks will lend without considering any debt outside of the SMSF; your super contributions are considered as income. Depending on your situation this may give you access to money that you can use to invest in property.

There are many rules around this type of investment and it is important to know you can only buy property through your SMSF if you comply with the rules. The property must:

— meet the 'sole purpose test' of solely providing retirement benefits to fund members

— not be acquired from a related party of a member

- not be lived in by a fund member or any fund members' related parties

- not be rented by a fund member or any fund members' related parties.

• • •

While these are all creative ways of leveraging and getting started, I am not advising you to take any particular option. What you need to do is go back to the plan and work out what you want to do and what you will need to get stuck into your renovation or build. This may mean working in one of the above ways or buying a more cost-effective property and building up your equity with each project.

The rest of the process takes a system and an action plan. It is in taking the action that we often see people get stuck. It is all well and good to have an idea, to think about your situation and make plans in your head. However, what I want to see is actions being put in place. It is my belief that the value is in the action, not the idea. So many people fall in love with the idea and don't take the actions required to realise that idea, rendering it worthless.

This means the real question you need to ask yourself is, 'What effort and resilience are you willing to invest to make this lifestyle happen?'

I am not suggesting you need to go all in, guns blazing, to make this happen. However, I feel I need to re-iterate that the validity of any of the above options will be 100 per cent in the execution and not in the idea of them.

At BuildHer, we know this is hard, and keeping up momentum alongside your already busy life can be stressful. This is why we share about the process. We have created a community and have mentors who have all been in your position before to help you through the process. It can be easy to get stuck and lose momentum while you are in it. We also know it is easy to feel overwhelmed before you begin and then never actually put anything you have learned into action.

Conclusion

Well, friends, we're nearly at the end of the book. Hopefully it's been a totally awesome journey and a useful learning experience for you.

To conclude, I'd like to look at what you need to know so you can get started if you fall over an amazing opportunity.

Build up your knowledge

Understand what type of deal you would consider looking at so you can work through what you would need to put together to make this happen. Create or join a community where you can sense check what you are working on. At BuildHer, we have an online community and fortnightly live sessions where people bring along their feasibilities and we review them. Sometimes, having to prepare to present a proposal can help you see the holes. In addition, if you have one that works it can be great to show it to others to see if they agree or see things that you haven't noticed yourself. Perspective is a wonderful thing.

Find a deal

Understand where your deal might come from and what you would need. For example, if you have identified that you need investors, will this be someone from your family, friends or other people you know? What information would they need and how can you know if this would be something they are interested in (or not)?

Create a clean and clear process

As in the example of a JV, will you buy first or put together the group first? What will be the trigger point? What information will you need to create this process? What case studies or processes can you delve into to access this information? If you are purchasing outright, what process would you need to go through, and how comfortable are you with this? Are there any necessities for you to be able to transact — for example, a 120-day settlement or a 5 per cent deposit?

Build up your documentation

Will this be a situation where you need legal contracts? Who will you use to set these up? For example, are you looking at doing pre-sale renovations like Kristen? If so, what are your thoughts about this? What scenarios do you need to play out and make clear so you are ready to go when the deal proceeds?

Understand your borrowing potential

Have a chat to your broker, or use BuildHer's broker — Entourage Finance — and let them know we referred you. Your broker should be able to give you a general idea of where you stand based on your current position over the phone if you have the right information at hand. Make sure you understand what type of documentation you will require so you can start gathering the necessary information. This will allow you to work through your next steps and what you are looking for in terms of the style of property.

A quick note here about always looking at a few different scenarios. For example, what if I move in with my parents and rent the property out while I am doing the planning phase? How much could I borrow then? Or, what if I got rid of my credit card and paid off the car finance? Or, what if I went back to work three days a week and my partner continued working fulltime? How much equity is there in our home that we could release? These are all equations: how will you know what to do if you don't know the implications?

Please remember this stuff is really fun if you let it be! There will always be things to learn, and the first few times will deliver the biggest learning curves.

I know that in some ways it's not easy and because it's not easy, not everyone is doing it. Some things you might find difficult are the renovations, taking the first steps and getting started, or thinking about creative ways to make your dollars stretch further, particularly in the beginning. The things you find hard, others may find easy — and vice versa.

There are so many skills that can be leveraged — some from inside the property and building world, and some from different industries that can be utilised within projects, bringing a fresh take to the game.

Don't focus too much on what other people are doing. The more you know about people, the more you understand that we are all bumbling along doing the best we can with the information we have on hand at the time. There is so much room for all of us to play in this space, particularly if we are playing together, leveraging our skills and helping each other.

• • •

For a copy of the spreadsheets or any other downloads, please visit: www.buildhercollective.com.au/bookfreebies

Acknowledgements

No-one does anything alone — and I certainly don't! I have much anxiety about forgetting to mention one of the many, many people who have supported me along the way.

John, my partner in life and building, whom I choose to love and live a fun and adventurous life with every day: writing this book has needed your support as it is all time that we are trading; time away from the growing kiddos, who are amazing and who are the inspiration for living our crazy life on our terms.

My mum, dad, sister and brother. I am one of the lucky ones. I have parents who challenge and help and push. They are the kind who embrace the effort and the attempt, not needing every aspect to be perfect or to pay off. The learning is the learning. This meant that when I came up with an idea, they were always quick to challenge and then jump in with support and love.

My dad, Big Mick — Grumpy (that's what his grandkids call him) — thank you for your ear, guidance and questioning. So many of the lessons I have learned came from you. My mum, Hurricane Helen, always attacking everything with enthusiasm and adventure, hard work, effort and determination combined with a selfless give. My sister: honestly, Caity is the best. She is one in a million and the reason I learned about joint ventures. If you had a family like this, you would know why I like JVs so much. And my brother, whose rivalry made me who I am today. See, I told you I was lucky.

Our team at BuildHer Collective. Present and past we have had so, so many amazing women who have helped us grow our community. Too many to list, but notably Rebecca, Rochelle, Meg, Jennifer, Rachel, Mel, Tamara, Sarah, Taeler — how lucky to be surrounded by incredible women all helping other women!

Our community — apparently we really need a community — is incredible! To all my fellow developers and DevelopHers, builders and BuildHers and friends in this community — too many to name. There is a generosity that I have seen throughout this industry that is unusual and should be celebrated. Thank you all for sharing with me so I might share with others.

A special thank you to Sandra, who edited this book, working through some jumbled messes to create a clear narrative.

A huge thank you to Lucy, Chris, Ingrid and Leigh from Wiley, in particular, who saw a need for this book as a resource and encouraged me to write it, even when I was having doubts. Even though I was a massive pain and had a few panicked moments in getting this done, you saw it through. I am unsure why I didn't know on the second book that it would be hard, but here we are. Thank you for your sightline and encouragement.

Dear Renovator,

How friggn exciting! What an adventure you are in for! This journey has been so crazy for us, however, I can say it is the one thing that has allowed us freedom of time and the ability to change and move with the season.

What a gift!

I hope you find the joy, creativity, freedom and profits across many facets of your life, just like we have.

Good luck!,

x Rebeka

P.S. If you need us reach out! we would love to help!

Index